BUILDING AN EFFECTIVE
LEADERSHIP TEAM
by

J.J. Turner D.Min.

QUALITY PUBLICATIONS
P.O. BOX 1060
ABILENE, TEXAS 79604
(915) 677-6262

ISBN: 0-89137-122-2

DEDICATION
To
Clyde Cope

A great brother in the Lord and an effective team member. Thank you for your encouragement.

BE THE BEST

If you can't be a pine on the top of a hill,
Be a scrub in the valley--but be
The best little scrub by the side of the rill:
Be a bush if you can't be a tree.

If you can't be a bush, be a bit of the grass,
Doing something for somebody's sake;
If you can't be a muskie, then just be a bass--
But the liveliest bass in the lake!

We can't all be captains, some have to be crew,
There's something for all of us here,
There's big work and little for people to do,
And the task we must do is the near.

If you can't be the highway, then just be a
trail,
If you can't be the sun, be a star;
It isn't by size that you win or you fail--
Be the best of whatever you are!

---Douglas Mulloch

4

CONTENTS

Section 3

TEAMWORK REQUIRES PLANNING

Section 4

FUNDAMENTALS FOR TEAM MEMBERS

PREFACE

A running back on a champion football team, after he had rushed for almost two hundred yards in a championship game, told an announcer: "I couldn't have done it without the rest of the team. The team won the game. That's all that matters!"

In all areas of life TEAMWORK makes the difference. Whether little teams like families, or big teams like the NFL, teamwork is the key to success or failure. This is especially true in the church.

It takes teamwork to get the work of the church done.

A dynamic, successful leadership team in the church doesn't just happen. It takes agreement on mission, selection, study, prayer, planning and work. Building an effective leadership team starts with individuals. When they are properly motivated and trained, they have the basics for being a productive team member.

God's army is never through with its leadership training. It merely moves from one phase to the next. There is always more to learn, as well as room for improving what we are now doing. "In-service training" is a must for the church.

This book is designed to help congregations develop and improve their leadership teams. It is divided into four major sections. Each section has a special contribution to make toward increasing leadership effectiveness. The sections may be studied in any sequence, or you may use the one that best fits your needs at the moment. This book is a manual for training men for greatness in the Kingdom of God.

J.J.Turner, D. Min.

8

INTRODUCTION

In 1886, Nevada had a State Fair. It was decided to have a contest among mule teams to see how much each team could pull. The first-place winners won by pulling 14,000 pounds. The second-place winners pulled 13,000 pounds. Someone then asked: "I wonder how much they could pull together. Added together, could they pull 27,000 pounds? They hitched up both teams, and the onlookers were staggered to see that it wasn't 27,000--It was 35,000 pounds!

We can multiply our accomplishments when we work as a team. Cooperation is an exciting must for progress.

A group of Army officers (60% said their decisions were made from self-interest rather than Army-interest (Sacramento **Bee**).

Leaders must be interested in **others** and work to reach the goals God has given us (Matthew 10:24).

Pat Riley, head coach of the L. A. Lakers basketball team said that a championship team is made up of members who love each other and care about one another (TV Lakers special, June 2, 1985).

If this is true of an NBA team, how much more is it true of God's championship team in the local church.

Coach Riley also said: "All can't be on stage or ride a white horse; some have to play supporting roles...it takes every man..."

That's just what the apostle Paul said in I Corinthians 12:13-27. It takes every member of the Body doing his/her job for the "team to win."

In this study we are going to look at some essential qualities of great teamwork. The teamwork we will be discussing is not just any old teamwork. We are talking about God's

9

work...our work with Him...our team efforts to accomplish His mission.

Team members come from various backgrounds. Thus, they must be molded together in order to be a productive group. This requires hard work and prayer.

It doesn't matter how long you have been a Christian, you are a member of the team in this congregation. You must discover where you fit. To help you in your discovery, God has placed helpers in the Body (cf. Ephesians 4:11-16).

The 13 sections of this study is designed to give you an overall view of teamwork and its relationship to the church. Please take the time to study it carefully and look up each Bible verse listed.

TEAMWORK MAKES THE DIFFERENCE

"The nice thing about teamwork is that you always have others on your side."

INTRODUCTION

"One of the greatest myths in sports is that a superstar can win alone...But business is not an individual game. Business is a team sport. Every CEO, no matter how brilliant, is utterly dependent on the commitment and teamwork of his players to win his games. No football player ever became a superstar without ten other guys on the field to make him one...I discovered that the critical factor in generating teamwork is to **get everyone involved.** All of us together, in business and in sports, are smarter than any one of us alone" (Fran Tarkenton, **Playing to Win**, pages 80, 81. Bantam Books, Copyright 1984).

What this record-setting Pro quarterback said has an application to teamwork in the church! God has placed us all on His team (1 Cor. 12:18).

I. THE IMPORTANCE OF TEAMWORK

A. It is essential in every area of society:
  1. Politics.
  2. Business.
  3. Sports.
  4. Religion.

B. The church is the most important area of all (Acts 20:28).

C. Illustration of two mules tied to a wagon and each is pulling in the opposite direction. (Together...but not teamwork).

II. MEANING OF TEAMWORK

   A. It is more than merely being on a team (Having a uniform doesn't make you a player).

   B. Webster's definition: "Two or more persons joined in a cooperative activity; teamwork is joint action by a group."
      1. A band is a team (Players must be in tune...)
      2. Husband and wife (Team).
      3. All are involved in teamwork of some kind...

   C. Bible Examples of Teamwork:
      1. Luke 5:10,11 (James, John and Simon were partners in fishing business... required teamwork).
      2. John 17:20,21 (Jesus' prayer for unity).
      3. 1 Cor. 3:9 ("Labourers together...").
      4. Heb. 4:6 ("People had a mind to work").
      5. Early church in the book of Acts.

III. BECOMING A TEAM MEMBER

   A. You are a member of the leadership team in the church:
      1. This is a very special work.
      2. Required much.

   B. How some became members (1 Cor. 12:12-27):
      1. Through desire (1 Tim. 3:1).
      2. Through reluctance (Pushed!).
      3. Through popularity contest.
      4. Through selection (Talents... preparation ... willing).
      5. Through response to needs.
      6. Through "Have to" reasons.

7. Respond to Bible command.

IV. **WHAT YOU BROUGHT TO THE TEAM** (All come from different points...):

A. Desire (To be a "Player").

B. Skills (Limited by education/ background/ Experiences).

C. Strengths (For assignments).

D. Weaknesses (Find task difficult).

E. Prejudices (Likes and Dislikes).

F. Temperament (Emotions... Self-control... fears... worries, etc.).

G. Influence (Each person has a circle of influence).

H. Attitudes (Phil. 2:5-8).

I. Knowledge (Bible/training).

J. Commitment (Matt. 16:24).

K. Willingness (Degrees).

L. Love (For God... others... church... self).

V. **EVERYTHING YOU BROUGHT TO THE TEAM IS NOW UNDER NEW MANAGEMENT**

A. You are now a SERVANT (Mark 10:45, like Jesus).

B. Committed to a singular goal (The work of God: Mark 16:15; Eph. 4:11-16).

C. Under the Lordship of Christ (Luke 6:46).

D. You/I have no right to apply "secular standards" to the things of God: Spiritual.

E. It operates through the "mind of Christ" (Phil. 2:5-8).

13

VI. HINDRANCES TO TEAMWORK

Teamwork is a constant challenge for leaders. It requires a deep desire to be content doing the work assigned to you. Without organized teamwork leaders will have problems in training and leading followers. Leaders must be aware of the possible enemies that may hinder teamwork. Some of the major ones are as follows:

A. A spirit of self-centeredness.

B. The leaders who have to be the "star performers."

C. A leader who is not considerate of others.

D. A leader who is not prepared to do his job.

E. A critical negative spirit.

F. By seeking the preeminent role, jobs, etc.

G. Being a loner.

H. Won't cooperate.

I. Spirit of fear takes over: Faith goes (12 spies, Num. 13, 14).

VII. ESSENTIALS TO TEAMWORK

A. A desire to cooperate with others. A desire to work for goals.

B. Must have confidence in God, Word and brethren.

C. Requires the best effort at all times.

D. Teamwork demands creativity.

E. Must have the spirit of a finisher (Not just a starter).

14

F. Love for one another. Patience will result.

G. Content with your part on the team.

H. Availability   (Manages his time).

I. Delegation (Give authority, plans, deadline and money to do job).

J. Constantly updating skills and knowledge.

K. Trust (Other team members).

L. Faith (Heb. 11:6).

VIII. GREAT TEAMWORK INVOLVES COMMUNICATIONS

"Anytime you have two persons talking about a problem, you have a conference." The ability to communicate effectively is one of the most useful skills a leader can possess. How skillful are you as a communicator?

A. Ten Suggestions For Good Communications:
   1. Clarify your ideas before communicating.
   2. Examine the TRUE PURPOSE of each communication.
   3. Consider the total physical setting whenever communicating.
   4. Consult with others (See your ideas from other's point of view).
   5. Be mindful of overtones as well as basic content.
   6. Take opportunity to convey something of value or help to the receiver.
   7. Follow up on communication.
   8. Communicate for tomorrow as well as for today.

9. Be sure your actions support your words.
10. Seek not only to be understood but to understand...LISTEN.

B. Remember these keys to retention as you seek to communicate:
1. We remember 20% of what we HEAR.
2. We remember 30 to 50% of what we SEE.
3. We remember 50 to 70% of what we HEAR and SEE.
4. We remember 70 to 80% of what we SEE, HEAR and SAY.
5. We remember 90% of what we SEE, HEAR, SAY and DO.

C. REMEMBER: A program is only as good as it is understood:

D. Why congregational communication is difficult:
1. Most people prefer remaining status quo.
2. People resist change.
3. Semantics create communication problems.
4. Preoccupation of thought is a major barrier.
5. "Curtain drawing" (Hearer shuts you out).
6. A negative spirit stops the message.
7. A lack of interest.
8. The "That's for others" attitude.
9. Drawing hasty conclusions without all the facts.
10. Mass sharing curtails communications (Always using the pulpit...person-to-person is best).

E. Five Stages of Getting an Idea Across:

Two researchers, Joe M. Bohlen and George M. Beal, in the Department of Economics and Sociology at Iowa State College, discovered that persons on farms go through five stages in accepting a new idea:

1. Awareness.
2. Interest.
3. Evaluation.
4. Trial.
5. Adoption.

IX. WHY BUILD A TEAM?

A. God is building teams (Eph. 4:11-16. In local churches).
   1. Men who are responsible for growth in the Body.
   2. "The fulness of Christ" (Maturity).

B. There is power in numbers (i.e., need at least two for a team):
   1. Two are better than one (Eccl. 4:9-11).
   2. Nehemiah said, "...half of my servants..." (Neh. 4:16,17).
   3. Jesus chose twelve (Matt. 10:1-5).
   4. Sent disciples out in pairs (Mark 6:7).
   5. Elders in the church (Tit. 1:5; 1 Tim. 3:1-7).
   6. Paul had helpers (Silas, John Mark, Barnabas).

C. Building a leadership team is essential to church growth:
   1. Numerical.
   2. Spiritual.
   3. Organizational.

D. Benefits of team membership:
   1. Team members are more identified

with (organizational) goals.
2. Being a team member gives a sense of being in control of your life.
3. Being a team member helps develop awareness of the complexities involved in a task.
4. Team membership fulfills many emotional needs: e.g.: self-esteem, feeling of acceptance, self-actualization, etc.
5. Team membership helps break down differences between members.
6. As a team member you have a chance to model what needs to be done.
7. Team members influence others. The more team members--the more influence.
8. Teams usually produce better decisions.
9. Rewards (Now--Eternity).
10. Living a productive life. Keeps you excited.

X. PERILS OF BEING A NEW TEAM MEMBER

A. Many men become team members without knowing what to expect. Sometimes they are surprised.
   1. The challenges of the new position.
   2. They have great desire and zeal.

B. Must realize these perils:
   1. There will be new time demands.
   2. Things may be moving too fast, or too slow.
   3. Expecting immediate change. People resist change.
   4. Disappointment with people not performing.

5. Rejection (By a few).
6. New experiences (Will face things never faced before).
7. Discouragement. Problems.
8. Isolation (Time alone).
9. Falling into the "I'll wait and see" attitude.
10. People won't/don't appreciate you and the work you do.
11. Possible conflicts with others (i.e., Peter and Paul).
12. Unfairness (May occur).

XI. SOME PRICELESS INGREDIENTS

A. Don't be afraid to make mistakes. They are okay. Sign of health and life.

B. Make an attitude adjustment every day (Prov. 23:7).

C. Dare dream.

D. Be enthusiastic about your work.

E. Pray for wisdom (James 1:5).

F. Be a booster (Heb. 10:24).

G. Be sold on being bold (Acts 4:11-13).

H. Develop spiritual toughness (Eph. 3:20; Rev. 2:10).

I. Live expectantly ("Something great will happen today...").

J. Carry your load.

K. Be a "Team member."

XII. PINPOINTING LEADERSHIP SKILLS

"I feel like a square peg in a round hole." This statement was made by a leader who was discussing his frustration over being assigned a job he didn't feel competent in.

A. All leaders don't have the same skills:
   1. In fact, it is because of differences that we are able to accomplish so many things for the Lord.
   2. Paul uses the human body to remind us of the complexities and uniqueness of each member of the church.
   3. There are many skills within the ranks of the local church's leadership team.

B. One of the tasks of leadership is to identify and implement the various skills possessed by members of the leadership team.
   1. In examining leadership teams, both within and without the church, a number of skills emerge as being essential for a group to reach a given objective.
   2. Leaders have to evaluate and find people who have the skills needed, then fit them into the team.

C. Some of the skills that blend together into a winning combination are as follows;
   1. **The idea man.** He can come up with "101" ideas.
   2. **Development man** (Can take idea and develop it).
   3. **Ability to implement** (once idea is developed).
   4. **Can sell the program**, etc. (Once it is developed).
   5. **Some men can maintain a project** once it is started.
   6. **Some men are good at evaluation.**
   7. **Problem solver.**

8. **Knowledge of Scripture** (Keep on biblical base).

D. One man, with rare exception, won't have all these skills:
1. One man may be a developer with some selling skills.
2. Another may be an idea man with some basic evaluation skills, etc.
3. When all skills are properly fitted together, like a puzzle, you will have a team which produces.

E. Not every program in the church will require the involvement of every skill on the leadership team.
1. The challenge is to find the right combination of skills needed for a specific task.
2. This means that leadership must know who has which skills.

F. According to a personal understanding of yourself and your abilities, which of the following skills do you believe you have in an UNUSUAL measure?

(Rate on a scale of 1 to 10, with 10 being the highest).

_____ I am an idea person.

_____ I can develop ideas.

_____ I am an implementor.

_____ I can sell a program or idea.

_____ I am good at maintaining.

_____ I am skilled in evaluating.

_____ I can solve problems.

_____ I have in-depth Bible knowledge.

QUALITIES OF AN
IDEAL TEAM MEMBER

Here are some characteristics and behaviors of leaders. From your point of view rank them in order of importance (e.g.: place a 1 beside the most important, etc).

____ Empathy

____ Role Model (Example)

____ Accessibility

____ Flexibility

____ Goal Setting

____ Positive thinker.

____ Servant's attitude.

____ Loyal

____ Spiritually minded

____ Finishes what he starts

____ Dependable

____ Gentleness

PERSONAL RESPONSE

1. Teamwork is important because...

2. The ideal team member is...

3. I want to be a better team member because...

4. Teamwork in our congregation is...

5. As a team member I expect...

6. Teamwork breaks down when...

7. Our team needs...

8. The three most important characteristics of a team are:

   (1)

   (2)

   (3)

9. "A team is no stronger than its weakest member." ( ) True ( ) False

10. A good example of teamwork is...

11. My greatest strength as a team member is...

12. As a team member I need...

13. As a team member I would like...

TEAM EFFECTIVENESS

To survive and grow in a congregation, there must be a "support system." An effective leadership team builds a Biblical Support System by developing open relationships and building trust. Ineffective teams always have unhealthy organizational support systems.

Characteristics of ineffective teams:

* Domination by the (a) leader(s)

* Warring cliques or subgroups

* Unequal participation or unequal use of group resources.

* Rigid or dysfunctional group norms and/or procedures.

* A climate of defensiveness or fear.

* Uncreative alternatives to problems

* Restricted communications

* Avoidance of differences or potential conflicts.

Effective teams work and pray to eliminate the "Characteristics" listed above.

THE TEAM CONCEPT

I. A team is a group of individuals with a _____ purpose and a _____ for accomplishing that purpose.

II. The team will accept the following:

1. Good management requires _____.

2. Group decisions are more _____.

3. Awareness is better than _____ of _____.

4. Consensus is better than _____.

5. No department can stand _____

6. An organization consists of _____ teams.

III. Team building efforts are characterized by:

1. _____ to the goals of the team.

2. _____ and _____ with open communication.

3. _____ and _____ among team members.

4. _____ team victories.

IV. Our team is

G_____

R _____

E _____

A _____

T _____

Determine Priorities Through Cooperation

Every enterprise has just so many re-
sources--time, money, leaders, facilities--with
which to do its work. These resources must
be used where they will count the most. This
will be accomplished only if the planning group
determines priorities. Here is an interesting
game that a planning group can play to sharpen
their skills in setting priorities:

Your party has just crash-landed on the
moon. You are about one hundred miles from
the life-support station which was your destin-
ation. Two members of your group have broken
arms. Other persons have numerous minor
cuts and scratches. With no problems you
can walk the distance in about four days.
The terrain is rugged. You can carry only
six items with you. Which items will you take?

1. A container of water
2. Evaporated milk
3. Moon compass
4. Two-way radio
5. Emergency oxygen tanks
6. First aid supplies
7. A rope
8. Small tent
9. Sleeping bags
10. A two-day supply of space food
11. Insulated oversuit
12. Tools for repairing backpack
13. A container of matches
14. Lantern
15. Pickax
16. Shovel
17. Flare gun and several flares
18. Combination heater and cooking stove
19. Camera
20. Binoculars
21. Map

Section 2

TEAMWORK WITH GOD

HOW TO WORK WITH GOD

INTRODUCTION

A. We have all seen signs or advertisements like these:
   1. "The Marines Are Looking For A Few Good Men."
   2. "Qualified Applicants Only."
   3. "Help Wanted."
   4. "Must Be Able To Deal With People..."
B. Every institution wants the very best people working for it:
   1. Human relations become key factors in job placement.
   2. Key question: "Can/does he get along well with people"?
   3. Most believe this is more important than a college degree.
C. God (needs) *wants* people too:
   1. Ezekiel 22:30: "And I sought for a man among them, that should make up the hedge and stand in the gap before me for the land, that I should not destroy it: but I found none."
   2. God could not find a man to work with Him. How sad!
   3. God is still looking for "Yet one man." A Micaiah (cf. 1 Kings 22:1-40).
D. Why does God (need) men?
   1. He has limited His work to earthen vessels (Romans 1:14-16).
   2. 2 Corinthians 4:7.
   3. Thus, not just any man will do. God doesn't search the ranks of the spiritually unemployed looking for volunteers. Jesus never called an idle man to follow Him.
   4. His work is challenging and demands dedicated workers. The best!

29

E. How did you learn HOW to work WITH God?
    1. By trial and error method (?).
    2. By following another leader (?).
    3. In a special school...college...seminar (?).
    4. By just doing the best I can...(?).

F. Some don't know HOW to work with God:
    1. They have been Christians for years and still don't know how to work with God.
    2. Every Christian must know HOW to work with God. This is eternally important.

G. Some are working against God:
    1. Matthew 6:24 ff (Can't serve two masters).
    2. The lukewarm are (Revelation 3:14-21).
    3. The unfruitful are (John 15:1-7; Galatians 5:18ff).
    4. The ignorant are (Hosea 4:6-8).
    5. The backsliders are (2 Peter 2:20,21).

H. Some confuse working WITH God with working FOR the brethren:
    1. See their work as merely another job.
    2. Must please the brethren (2 Timothy 4:1-5).
    3. Their great concern is about "What will they think?"
    4. Truth: We do work WITH God and with one another.

I. Some mistake programs for working WITH God:
    1. Lose sight of purpose and mission of church (If they ever knew).
    2. Think programs are in the Bible (Men develop programs).

(3) Will fight for traditions but not for God (Mark 7:2,7,9).

4. God may not be in/for a program.

J. Some think working with God is seasonal ("When I want to...").
1. "Four hours per week" (4 church services).
2. "In season and out of season" (2 Timothy 4:1-5).
3. No vacations from God and His work.
4. Christianity is LIFE not merely a WAY of life (John 10:10).

K. In this series of studies we are going to study some relevent truth about HOW to work with God.

I. **GOD NEEDS MEN WHO CAN/WILL WORK WITH HIM**

A. A Person may know "101 things":
1. He may know Theology, Greek, Hebrew, Psychology, Methods, etc.
2. And still not be able to work WITH God. Why? He doesn't know how.
3. Spiritual work is not like any other *mission* work. It requires God's methods. *vision*

B. The Bible makes it clear that we are workers WITH God:
1. 2 Corinthians 6:1: "We then as workers together with him."
2. 1 Corinthians 3:9: "For we are labourers together WITH God..."
3. One plants, another waters, and God gives the increase (1 Corinthians 3:6-8).

C. Some want to work with God on their conditions:
(1). Luke 9:57-62.
(2) Luke 14:15-24.

D. The Prophet Jonah is a good example of a man who didn't want to work with God (On His conditions):
   1. God gave Jonah a command to go preach repentance to Nineveh (Jonah 1:1-4),
   2. He ran away from his assignment (Read the book of Jonah).

E. It takes preparation to work WITH God:
   1. The disciples were trained for 3 1/2 years by the Lord. It has been estimated He was with them for more than 10,000 hours.
   2. The Holy Spirit came to complete the training job begun by Jesus.
   3. Our task, too, is to train faithful men (2 Timothy 2:2).
   4. Example: Kind of workers God needs (Exodus 18:21 ff).

II. JESUS WORKED WITH THE FATHER

A. He was about His Father's business (Luke 2:49). What was His business/work?

John 5:17, 19-20, 30

   1. Save from sin (Matthew 1:21; Luke 19:10).
   2. Serve people (Mark 10:45; cf. John 13:4-16).
   3. Be an example (1 Peter 2:21).
   4. Die for sins (Matthew 26:28; Galatians 1:4).
   5. Suffer for mankind (John 12:27).
   6. Give abundant life (John 10:10).
   7. Preach (Mark 1:38).
   8. Fulfill law (Matthew 5:17).
   9. Call sinners to repentance (Matthew 9:13).
   10. Suffer for men (John 12:27; 1 Peter 3:18, 4:1,2).

B. He came to do His Father's will (work). In John 17 we read HOW:
1. "I have glorified thee on earth" (v. 4).
2. "Finished thy work" (v. 4).
3. "Manifested thy name" (v. 6).
4. "Given them thy words" (v. 8).
5 "Kept them" (v. 12).
6. "Given them thy word" (v. 14).
7. "Sent them into the world" (v. 18).
8. "Given them thy glory" (v. 22).
9. "Known them" (v. 25).
10. "Declared thy Name" (v. 26).

C. "My meat is to FINISH his work" (John 4:34):
1. No thought of quitting.
2. John 5:36; 9:4; 10:25.
3. John 5:17.
4. "It is finished."

D. We, too, must work with/for the Father!

III. **JESUS TAUGHT ABOUT WORK (John 3:1,2; 6:66-68).**

A. **Jesus taught by word and actions:**
1. Men were to hear Him (Matthew 17:5).
2. John 17:17; 1:17.

B. **Taught worker worthy of wages (Rewards):**
1. Matthew 10:10. "...the workman is worthy of his meat."
2. Law of reaping and sowing (Gal. 6:5-8).

C. **Workers of iniquity:**
1. Luke 13:27: "..depart...all ye workers of iniquity."

33

2. Not all workers have right attitude: EVIL.

D. **Parable of Sower**:
1. Used worker to demonstrate point.
2. Luke 8:5-15
3. Taught varied results from efforts. Depends on hearts.

E. **Judgment relates to works/deeds**:
1. Matthew 25:31-46
2. Works of love and compassion (Luke 16:19-31).

F. **Sent forth workers**: (Taught by example):
1. The 70 (Luke 10:1-7).
2. The 12 (Matthew 10:1-5).

G. **Taught against idleness**:
1. Matthew 20:,1-16; esp. v. 6
2. Must work while it is still day!

IV. **PAUL TAUGHT ABOUT WORKS**

A. He mentioned it many times in Timothy and Titus:
1. 1 Timothy 2:10; 3:1; 5:10; 5:25; 6:18.
2. 2 Timothy 2:21; 3:17.
3. Titus 1:16; 2:7, 14; 3:1,8,14.

B. Was a worker:
1. 1 Corinthians 15:10.
2. 2 Corinthians 12:9, 10.
3. Colossians 1:28, 29
4. Ephesians 3:4, 5.

V. **DOERS/WORKERS ARE BLESSED**
A. There are some people who are nonproductive (James 2:14-26):
1. See a need (v. 15).
2. Won't do anything but talk (v. 16-19).

34

3. This approach is vain (v. 20).

B. Our work is not in vain when we do it:
   1. 1 Corinthians 15:58.
   2. He blesses His work!

C. Fruits come from effort (Colossians 1:10, 11).

D. Abounding in work--grace (2 Corinthians 9:8).

E. Will hear, "Well done..." (Matthew 25:21).

F. Must be DOERS (James 1:19-23).

VI. GOD KNOWS OUR WORKS

A. "I know thy works" (Message from Christ to 7 churches of Asia): Rev. 2:2; 2:9; 2:13; 2:19; 3:1; 3:8; 3:15.
   1. Read Revelation chapters 2 & 3.

B. God works in us:
   1. Philippians 2:12,13; Ephesians 3:20.
   2. Therefore, He knows what we are doing.

C. We can't hide from God:
   1. Psalm 139:1-12
   2. He sees and knows all. There are no secrets.

D. What does He see when He looks at your works?

E. Back to Genesis 6: "He saw the wickedness of man."

F. Some people are more concerned with others seeing their works than they are with God seeing them:

35

1. This is wrong attitude.

VII. SOME EXAMPLES OF HOW SOME HAVE WORKED WITH GOD

A. **Abraham** (Father of the faithful):
1. God called Abraham to work WITH Him (Genesis 12:1-3).
2. Abraham obeyed God (Genesis 12:4ff).
3. Abraham's faith was tested (Genesis 22).
4. He worked WITH God all the days of his life (Hebrews 11:8-19).

B. **Moses** (The great prophet/leader):
1. God called him (Exodus 3 & 4).
2. He obeyed God (Exodus 6-12).
3. He was a leader in difficult times.
4. He lived by faith (Hebrews 11:23-29).

C. **The Prophets in Israel:**
1. Jeremiah (Book of Jeremiah. He preached 40 years without a response; yet, he continued to work WITH God).
2. Isaiah (cf. Isaiah 6:1-12).
3. Amos (Preached to a sinful people. See book of Amos).
4. Nehemiah (Led God's people in rebuilding the walls; Neh. 4:6).
5. Elijah (2 Kings 1 & 2; 1 Kings 17-19).

D. **John the baptist:**
1. He prepared the way for the Lord (Matthew 3:1-14).
2. He gave his life in service to God (Matthew 14).

E. **Jesus worked with the Father:**
1. At an early age He was about His

Father's business (Luke 2:49).
2. John 9:4; 17:4,5.
3. Philippians 2:5-8 (He **gave** Himself for service).

F. **The apostle Paul**:
1. He knew How to work with God.
2. 2 Timothy 3:10-12).
3. He worked until his death (2 Timothy 4:5-8).

VIII. **WE ARE CREATED FOR GOOD WORKS**:
A. **Example**:
1. Sun was created to shine.
2. The vine was created to bear fruit.
3. The eye was created to see.
4. We are created to work for God.

B. **The Bible makes this clear**:
1. Ephesians 2:8-10.
2. 2 Corinthians 9:8.

C. **We provoke each other to work**:
1. Hebrews 10:24.
2. One reason for assembly.

D. **We must abound in good works**:
1. 1 Cor. 15:58.
2. "More than merely get by."

E. **Must be fruitful in every good work.**
1. Colossians 1:10-11.
2. God wants results.

F. **Faith works**:
1. Gal. 5:6,13,14.
2. Action is faith's expression (cf. Hebrews 11).

G. **Every member works**:
1. Ephesians 4:15,16.
2. 1 Corinthians 12:13-27.
3. Everyone has unique abilities.

IX. WHY WE WORK:

A. **Because of needs:**
1. The world is lost (1 John 5:19).
2. People have needs (Jas. 1:27; Gal. 6:10).

B. **To obey God's commandments:**
1. Luke 6:46.
2. John 14:15.

C. **Because of Love:**
1. Galatians 5:6,13,14.
2. For God, others and self.

D. **Glorify God:**
1. Revelations 4:11 (KJV: Bring God pleasure).
2. 1 Peter 4:11.

E. **For good report:**
1. Women (1 Timothy 5:9,10).
2. People see what you do.

F. **It produces results:**
1. Fruit (John 15:1-9).
2. Matthew 3:8.

G. **It brings joy and happiness:**
1. Acts 20:35.
2. Begins with elders, etc.
3. Crown of life (Rev. 2:10).

H. **Our work is greater!**
1. John 14:12-14.
2. Spiritual: Teach, baptize, etc.

I. **Doers blessed.**
1. James 1:22.
2. James 1:25.
3. James 5:19-20.

X. THERE ARE VARIOUS KINDS OF WORKERS.

A. **Some Good:**
   1. Worthy of wages (Matthew 10:10).
   2. An unashamed worker (2 Tim. 2:15).
   3. Fellow-worker (partner) (Rom. 12:21; 2 Cor. 6:1).
   4. Productive.

B. **Some bad:**
   1. Workers of iniquity (Luke 13:27).
   2. Deceitful workers (2 Cor. 11:13).
   3. Evil workers (Phil. 3:2).

C. **Procrastinators:**
   1. Sitting and waiting.
   2. John 4:34-37 ("say not...").

D. **Unskilled:**
   1. New converts (1 Peter 2:1,2).
   2. By reason of time (Hebrews 5:12-14).

E. **Real Active:**
   1. The early Christians (Book of Acts).
   2. Paul's friends and fellow-workers (Romans 16:1-23).

F. **Unprofitable workers:**
   1. Matthew 25:14-30, esp. v. 30.
   2. God expects us to use our minds.

XI. **FIGURES THAT SUGGEST WORK:**

A. **Soldiers:**
   1. 2 Timothy 2:1-5.
   2. Requires training, discipline and work.

B. **Farmer:**
   1. 2 Timothy 2:6.
   2. Patience and hard work.

C. **Runner:**

       1. 1 Corinthians 9:24,26.
       2. Endurance to finish.

D. **Boxer:**
       1. 2 Timothy 4:7.
       2. 1 Timothy 6:12.

E. **Wrestler:**
       1. Ephesians 6:12.
       2. Rough and painful.

F. **Builders:**
       1. 1 Corinthians 3:10.
       2. Plans, cost, work.

G. **Laborers:**
       1. 1 Corinthians 3:9.
       2. Common tasks.

H. **Servants:**
       1. Colossians 3:24.
       2. Galatians 5:13.

I. **Worker:**
       1. 2 Corinthians 6:1.
       2. Busy.

J. **Fisherman:**
       1. Mark 1:17.
       2. Training, patience, diligence.

K. **Stewards** (Managers):
       1. 1 Corinthians 4:1,2.
       2. Manage the affairs of God.

L. **Human body:**
       1. Ephesians 4:15,16.
       2. 1 Corinthians 12:12-27.

XII. **GOD NEEDS MEN WHO PRACTICE WHAT THEY PREACH/TEACH**

A. Credibility is the challenge of our times:
       1. We are constantly confronted

messenger & message

by manipulators who try to use the media to control us.

    2. Many politicians say what people want to hear.

    3. Most public speaking is for money or pleasure.

B. Credibility is critical in religion:

    1. You don't notice if a druggist is a good father, pays his bills, or is kind. You just want him to fill your prescription.

    2. The gospel message, however, is mixed with the man. It is the only work where you can't separate the message from the messenger.

C. If teacher/preacher doesn't live what he preaches, people won't believe what he preaches:

    1. Preach peace..on drugs for his nerves, etc.

    2. Preach do...won't do anything.

    3. Preach go...but stays.

    4. Preach don't worry...but does.

D. The power of example is awesome:

    1. "What you are speaks so loudly I can't hear what you are saying."

    2. We are "light, salt," etc.

XIII. **GOD NEEDS MEN WHO ARE WILLING TO BE LIKE THEIR LORD**

A. He was a servant of all (Philippians 2:5-8).

B. He taught about being a servant (Matthew 10:24-26).

C. He came to be a servant (Mark 10:45).

D. 1 Peter 4:11 (Suffer as a Christian).

E. He loved and gave (Romans 5:6-9).

F. This means having the right attitude (Proverbs 23:7; Philippians 2:5).

G. Die faithfully (Revelation 2:10).

XIV. HOW TO WORK WITH GOD

(There are many things involved in working with God. There are several cardinal points which must be followed if you hope to work WITH God. You work WITH God by...:)

A. **Most Jobs Have:**
   1. Job description
   2. Regulations
   3. Accountability
   4. Benefits
   5. Training
   6. Objectives
   7. Satisfaction
   8. Challenge--problems.

B. **Can Forget God**
   1. Psalm 44:20   Name
   2. Isaiah 17:10   Salvation
   3. Jeremiah 3:20
   4. Ezekiel 23:35
   5. Hosea 8:24   Maker

C. **Knowing Him:** (Jeremiah 31:31)
   1 He must not be a stranger to you.
   2. Eternal life is based upon knowing God (John 17:3).
   3. Know Him through word (John 8:32); and through nature (Romans 1:18-21).

D. **Starting right:**
   1. You must be "born again" (John 3:1-5).
   2. Spiritual work involves spiritual

people (Romans 8:6).

E. **By listening to Him:**
   1. Psalm 85:8 - John 1:17; Rom. 10:17
   2. He knows what **we need**...what we **must do**...how we must act, etc.

F. **Thinking His thoughts:**
   1. We are prone to think carnal thoughts.
   2. Isaiah 55:6-11.

G. **Obeying His commands:**
   1. Luke 6:46; Revelation 22:14.
   2. Hebrews 5:8,9 (This is following Jesus' example).

H. **Trusting His word:**
   1. John 1:17; 17:17.
   2. Only the truth will free (John 8:32,36).

I. **Being holy in your lifestyle:**
   1. 1 Peter 1:15 ("Be holy as he is holy").
   2. This means we must be "different" (Romans 12:1,2).

J. **Honoring priorities:**
   1. Knowing what is FIRST in my life.
   2. The Kingdom of God (Matthew 6:33).

K. **Seeking His will in all things:**
   1. "Not my will...but thine..." (Matthew 16:24).
   2. James 4:15 ("If the Lord will").

L. **Loving all people:**
   1. John 3:16.
   2. Even our enemies. The brethren.

M. **Being a faithful steward:**

1. We manage God's property.
2. 1 Corinthians 4:1,2.

N. **Studying His word:**
   1. 2 Timothy 2:15; 3:15-17; Hosea 4:6-8
   2. This requires time and effort.

O. **Acknowledging Him as Supreme:**
   1. There are no other gods before Him (Exodus 20:1-15).
   2. Isaiah 6:1-6.

P. **Living and working by faith:**
   1. Hebrews 11:6.
   2. James 1:2-5.
   3. Must not walk by sight.
   4. "This is work of God that ye believe" (John 6:29)

Q. **Not walking after the flesh:**
   1. Romans 8:1-12.
   2. We live in a spiritual kingdom (Colossians 1:11-16).
   3. Galatians 5:18-20.

R. **By thinking spiritually about spiritual things**
   1. Romans 8:6
   2. Colossians 3:1,2.
   3. Worldly thinking isn't Biblical thinking.

S. **By cooperating with other members of the Body:** (Isa. 2:2-4) "All nations"
   1. 1 Corinthians 12:12-27.
   2. Ephesians 4:11-16.
   3. Luke 10:2 "Harvest great..few labourers."
   4. Must be a "team" person.

T. **Not following blind leaders:**
   1. Matthew 15:13,14.
   2. Jesus will always lead us properly.

U. **Praying for wisdom from above:**
   1. 1 Thessalonians 5:17.
   2. James 1:5; 3:17,18.

V. **Discipling others in our world:**
   1. Matthew 28:18-20.
   2. Luke 19:10 (Seeking the lost...like Jesus did).

W. **Developing your gifts and talents:** (potential to be like Christ).
   1. Romans 12:3-16
   2. Ephesians 4:11-16.
   3. God only requires you to use what you have.

X. **Denying self:** (after baptism--what now?)
   1. Matthew 16:24.
   2. Keep on following Him daily.

Y. **Helping those who are in need:**
   1. James 1:27.
   2. Galatians 6:10; 2 Corinthians 8&9.

Z. **By producing the fruits of the Spirit:**
   1. Galatians 5:18-ff.
   2. This is a must for every Christian.

AA. **By being about the Father's business.**
   1. Luke 2:49
   2. Must use His methods.

BB. **Must be Bold in Working.**
   1. Acts 4:13.
   2. Prov. 28:1 "Bold as a Lion"

CC. **By Having a Sense of Destiny:**
   1. Esther 4:14
   2. "My hour has come"

DD. **By being zealous**
   1. Psa. 69:9; John 2:17.
   2. Titus 2:14.

3. Eccl. 9:10 "Hand, might"

CONCLUSION

A. God needs men (and women) to work with Him:
    1. His needs are more important than anyone's in the universe.
    2. His work, through man, is the salvation of souls.
    3. We must never forget this truth.

B. God needs men like:
    1. Philip...to send to a lost eunuch (Acts 8:26-40).
    2. Peter...to send to a Cornelius (Acts 10).
    3. Ananias...to send to Saul (Acts 22:7-19).

C. God needs men with beautiful feet (Romans 10:13-17).

D. Are you working with God, or are you working against Him?
    1. Are you willing to learn?
    2. Begin today: "...The harvest truly is great, but the labourers are few..." (Luke 10:2).

E. We have a **reason** for being on earth:
    1. For others "to see our good works..." (Matt . 5:16).
    2. Bring God pleasure (Rev. 4:11 KJV).
    3. Are you fulfilling your purpose for existing?

Section 3

TEAMWORK REQUIRES PLANNING

GROWTH THROUGH PLANNING

"Failure to plan is planned failure."
"People step aside for a person with a plan."
"Make no small plans because they don't have the power to excite."

INTRODUCTION

A. For the church to fulfill her mission, leaders must pray and plan.

   1. The greatest work under heaven must not be left to chance or accident.
   2. We are where we are today because of our plans (or lack of plans).

B. The world moves on plans:

   1. An Apollo moon shot.
   2. A trip to Hawaii.
   3. A small business meeting.

C. The church, too, moves on plans.

   1. Preaching the gospel to the world requires a plan.
   2. Reaching your community requires a plan.
   3. Personal growth requires a plan.

D. What do we mean by **planning**?

   1. Definition: "Planning is the process of predetermining a course of action."
   2. It is preparing a map for "the trip."
   3. It is to move with purpose.
   4. It is making preparation before you begin.

E. In this lesson we will study some fundamental truths relative to planning in the local church.

I. **Planning Is Biblical**

  A. God Planned:
    1. Long-range:
      a. To save man before the foundation of the world (Eph. 1:3-7).
      b. To bring the Messiah into the world (Genesis 3:15; Gal. 4:4).
      c. To make a great nation of Abraham's seed (Genesis 12:1-3; 13:16).
      d. To establish His Kingdom (Isa. 2:2-4).
    2. Short-range:
      a. Bring a flood in Noah's day (Genesis 6)
      b. Destroy Tower of Babel (Genesis 11:1-9).
    3. Isaiah 14:24 (RSV) "The Lord of hosts has sworn; As I have planned, so shall it be and as I have purposed, so shall it stand."

  B. Jesus Planned.
    1. Long-Range (Matt. 24:1-32)
    2. Intermediate Plans (His burial and resurrection)
    3. Short-range (Mark 1:38).

  C. All prophecy, as a rule, is an illustration of planning.

  D. Some Bible teaching on Planning:
    1. Luke 14:28-30 (plan to build).
    2. Proverbs 16:3 ("...your plans will be established")
    3. 1 Cor. 14:40 (Do properly and in

order).
4. Psalm 32:8; 37:23.
5. Luke 24:47; Acts 1:8 (Plan for spread of the Gospel).

II. **Three Types of Planning**

A. Long-range (3, 5, 10 or more years). Some Benefits are:
1. Enables you to set priorities.
2. Gives lead time to prepare for future actions.
3. Ensures lack of surprises.
4. Enables you to develop strategies.

B. Short-range (1 to 3 years)
1. Help translate long-range into reality.
2. Yearly calendar of events, budget, those who serve lists, etc., are short range.

C. Operational planning.
1. Weekly activities
2. Monthly activities.
3. Quarterly activities.

D. All three are interrelated.

III. **Six Major Objectives of Planning.**

A. The following objectives should be taken into account when you plan:
1. Planning must take into consideration **WHAT** should be done.
2. Planning must decide **WHY** it should be done.
3. Planning determines **WHERE** it should be done.
4. Planning determines **WHO** should do it.
5. Planning decides **WHEN** it should

be done.

6. Planning decides **HOW** it should be done.

B. Use this information as a planning base:

1. Answer each question.
2. Will give order and save time.

IV. Some **Mechanics of Planning**

A. WE MUST MAKE AN HONEST SELF APPRAISAL
(This can be accomplished by asking the following questions:)

1. Where do we presently stand?
2. What are our assets and liabilities?
3. What are our present goals? Spiritually? Physically?
4. Do we have any definitive aims?
5. What are our short-range goals?
6. What are our long-range goals?
7. Are our goals tangible or intangible at this time?
8. Are we motivated?
9. Are we working diligently?
10. Is there a spirit of cooperation?
11. Are we enthusiastic?
12. Have we been successful in the past?

B. WE MUST FOCUS OUR THINKING AND PLANNING ON SPECIFICS.

1. We must plan immediate goals as well as long range ones.
2. We must remember, "Low aims is only self-concept expressing itself." Aim high!
3. We must be specific in our goals. We must write them down.
4. We must dedicate ourselves with singleness of heart to reach these

51

goals.

5. Each person involved must have a personal plan of action. Do you have one?

C. WE MUST DEVELOP A PLAN FOR REACHING OUR GOALS.

1. A detail map must be drawn with the "how" to get there stated very clearly.

2. We must set a deadline for reaching the goal(s).

3. We must list ALL possible obstacles to our goal and how to get around them.

4. We must pinpoint our strength, weakness, assets and liabilities. We must determine where we are and where we want to go.

5. We must see every problem as a challenge.

6. With God's help we CAN DO all things. We cannot fail!!

D. WE MUST HAVE A SINCERE DESIRE FOR THE LORD'S WORK TO SUCCEED.

1. This will give added strength for reaching the goals.

2. Try to encourage each member of the congregation to examine himself and ask: (a) What are the obstacles I must overcome for the plan to work? (b) What are the plans? Do I know them all? (c) What are the rewards? (d) Is it worth it?

E. WE MUST MAINTAIN CONFIDENCE IN GOD AND BRETHREN.

1. Confidence submits itself to obstacles and overcomes them.

2. Confidence stimulates creative imagination. We will never do it until we think we can.
3. Confidence, therefore, in God and brethren will guarantee success.
4. "We either succeed at failure, or succeed to success."
5. "Will we think big or will we think small?" Confidence will determine!

F. WE MUST DEVELOP DETERMINATION TO FOLLOW THROUGH WITH PLANS.

1. No matter what others do, I will follow through.
2. No matter what they think, I will follow through.
3. No matter what obstacles arise, I will follow through.
4. I know that it is easy to make plans, but hard to follow through.
5. It is easy to get excited in a crowd, or at a pep talk. But to succeed in the long run, there must be constant personal MOTIVATION. Do you have it?

G. WE MUST REMEMBER THE PITFALLS.

1. Considering financing to be the first step.
2. Determining the personnel or facilities BEFORE the program is written.
3. Failure to creatively involve the kinds of people necessary to do the jobs.
4. Failure to secure proper help and staffing.

V. BRAINSTORMING AND PLANNING

A very important tool in planning is brainstorming. Webster defines brainstorming as, "the unrestrained offering of ideas by all members of a group meeting as in a business planning conference." From such a session comes many valuable benefits.

A. VALUE OF BRAINSTORMING.

1. Involves each person in the group. (The shy person will find himself involved before he knows it.)
2. Promotes enthusiasm and excitement (The many possibilities will be encouraging.)
3. Stimulates the minds of all present (Will help to draw from subconscious).
4. Produces many new ideas that are good and worthwhile (It will also revive old ideas).
5. Promotes creativity and use of imagination.
6. Important key in achieving success.
7. Several heads are better than one.

B. SOME GUIDELINES FOR BRAINSTORMING

1. Be sure each participant understands the purpose of a brainstorming session.
2. Do not criticize anyone's comment (This is not the purpose of brainstorming. Let each person speak freely.
3. Be spontaneous (Say what you think).
4. Seek as much quantity as possible (50 ideas are better than 15).
5. Build upon the ideas of others (Their comments will provoke deeper thoughts and better ideas).
6. Record all ideas that are presented

(May be done in writing, tape recorder).
7. Set a time limit (The pressure of time produces results. An open-end session will drag on and on).
8. Have a leader (chairman) to direct the session.
9. At a later date evaluate the ideas one by one (Select a committee. Don't neglect a single idea).
10. Never conclude that a problem or need is too small for brainstorming. It will amaze you at the things that may be brought out relative to a so-called unimportant problem (We are not advocating that brainstorming be reduced to an exercise in trivials).
11. State each problem as clearly as possible. Be sure it is fully understood.
12. Present and storm one idea or problem at a time (Do not get side-tracked).
13. Present any known data you may have relative to the subject.
14. All participants must readily identify with the issue under storming.
15. Statements relative to the issue must not be taken personally by another participant.
16. The leader should launch the session, if possible, by presenting one or two ideas. (Or he may simply state the problem.).
17. Pray for wisdom (James 1:2-5).

C. Add brainstorming to your planning sessions. It will produce results that you will be pleased with. It is a must for good planning.

VI. Some MUSTS For Planning:

A. Don't forget these 20 rules when planning:

1. Always plan beyond what you can do in your own strength. (Walk by faith--not sight.)
2. Make sure the plan will bring God glory.
3. Don't count your money before you make your plans. Make your plans and then **count** on God to provide.
4. Never say NO to a good idea or a commandment of God.
5. Trust God no matter what happens or doesn't happen. (Nehemiah 6:16).
6. Pray for wisdom (James 1:5).
7. Expect plans to change.
8. Develop the resources (manpower, programs, facilities, etc.).
9. Make all planning a TEAM effort. Get ideas from others.
10. Be sure you have a clear set of policies and procedures.
11. Keep your mind set on things above (Colossians 3:1,2; Rom. 12:1, 2).
12. Don't quit.
13. Establish standards for evaluation.
14. Coordinate all efforts.
15. Remember plans aren't the end, merely means.
16. Keep it simple.
17. Beware of traditions.
18. Be flexible.
19. Stay positive.
20. Set personal goals.

B. Form people into committees:

1. Choose from all age groups.

2. Clarify the objectives each committee is to accomplish.
3. Let them form tentative goals and action plans.

VII. How to Start Planning.

A. Study your Bible:
1. The mission of the church:
   a. Evangelism (Mark 16:15, 16)
   b. Edification (Eph. 4:11-16)
   c. Benevolence (Gal. 6:10; Jas. 1:27).
   d. Bring God glory (Rom. 4:11 KJV).
2. Affirm your commitment to these goals.

B. Take a congregational survey: "What Should Our Church Do Next Year?"

Select what you think should be the eight key emphases of our church during the coming year. Then rate according to importance, 1, 2, 3, etc. The most important items to you may not be listed. If so, make your own suggestions at the end of this sheet and rate them in the overall total.

___ 1. Stronger church fellowship.
___ 2. More vital worship services.
___ 3. Strengthened counseling ministry.
___ 4. Enlarged staff.
___ 5. Enlarged and more coordinated church committees.
___ 6. Better financial program.
___ 7. More effective fellowship with other churches.
___ 8. Deacons doing more in the life of the church.

___ 9. Enlarged Sunday School and strengthened Bible teaching program.
___ 10. Stronger evangelism program to the unsaved.
___ 11. Enlarged and strengthened training program.
___ 12. Enlarged and strengthened music program.
___ 13. Stronger mission emphasis.
___ 14. More stress on family life and family problems.
___ 15. Stronger youth program.
___ 16. Better church discipline.
___ 17. Deeper spiritual life for church membership.
___ 18. Enlistment of inactive church members
___ 19. Establishment of a new mission church.
___ 20. Enlarged ministry of the church library.
___ 21. Ministry to alcoholics.
___ 22. More participation in the poverty programs of the community.
___ 24. Ministry to the deaf.
___ 25. Ministry to college students and students in vocational training.
___ 26. Ministry to the mentally retarded.
___ 27. Greater use of the talents of the membership.
___ 28. More emphasis on prayer life.
___ 29. Stronger program of leadership development
___ 30. New buildings
___ 31. Better parking facilities
___ 32. Better supervision and maintenance of church building

and property.
___ 33. More stress on democracy in conducting church affairs.
___ 34. Better communication among groups in the church
___ 35. More adequate office facilities
___ 36. _____
___ 37. _____
___ 38. _____

CONCLUSION

There is a great work to be done by the Lord's people. The ever vital question is **HOW** to accomplish this work. Much study, prayer, sacrifice and planning must go into it; especially, by the leadership. Goals must be set with an organized plan for reaching them. This will require many long hours of hard work. But it is worth it because it involves the greatest work in the world.

In closing, the following words by Daniel H. Burnham, former Chicago architect and city planner, reminds us of the challenge before us:-
"Make no little plans; they have no magic to stir men's blood and probably themselves will not be realized. Make big plans; aim high in hope and work; remembering that a noble, logical diagram once recorded will never die, but long after we are gone will be a living thing, asserting itself with ever-growing insistency. Remember our sons and grandsons are going to do things that would stagger us. Let your watchword be order and your beacon beauty. Think big. Remember that when you create a situation that captures the imagination, you capture life, everything."

Words like WORLD, EVERY CREATURE,

HEAVEN, ETERNAL LIFE, HELL, etc., remind us that our Lord has taught us to THINK BIG. Therefore, we must PLAN and act accordingly.

BIBLIOGRAPHY

Leadership and Church Growth, J. J. Turner (Quality Publications, P.O. Box 1060, Abilene, Tx. 79604).

Christian Leadership Handbook, J. J. Turner. (Howard Publishing Company, 1979, 107 Yellowood, West Monroe, La. 71291).

Section 4

FUNDAMENTALS FOR TEAM MEMBERS

Chapter 1

THE IMPORTANCE OF LEADERSHIP TRAINING

I recently received a letter from a frustrated brother which contained this paragraph: "...I spoke with a few of them at length...One man said, 'We never really have looked beyond a year or so in the future.' Another said, 'You are interested in leadership training while another is interested in...' I guess I took too much for granted when I brought up the subject of leadership. I thought that all of them recognized the need for learning more on how to be leaders. How can any Christian not see the need of leadership training...?"

This letter is just one of many examples of how difficult it is to get some members of the church to see the need for leadership training. Congregations across the land are suffering because leadership training is being neglected. They drift from week to week, content with remaining status quo. A few are ready to close their doors; others are riddled with problems; some don't know what to do next, etc.

It's amazing how we recognize the fact that we are in the Lord's army and at the same time act as though we don't need any training. No wonder we are losing some major battles in our day. The church must be constantly preparing for her war with the forces of evil (cf. Ephesians 6:11-18). Every soldier must be prepared to march forward for the Captain of his salvation.

To underscore the importance of leadership training, I offer the following reasons why leadership and leadership training is so essential in our day.

First, the local congregation is in its present position because of its leadership. This is a hard truth for some brethren to accept. Our location tomorrow is being determined by what is done (or not done) today.

Second, God's work, which is the greatest in the world, must not be left to chance. It is rare for an army to win a battle by accident. Victory comes from planning and hard work. We must not depend upon the "stumbling method" of leadership.

Third, God's word exemplifies the importance of leadership. Two outstanding Old Testament examples are Moses and Isaiah (cf. Exodus 18:13-23; Isaiah 6:1-6). The New Testament clearly sets forth the need for elders to be prepared (cf. 1 Timothy 3:1-7; 1 Peter 5:1-5). Evangelists and deacons also need preparation (cf. 2 Timothy 2:2; 1 Timothy 3:8-13). Jesus spent more than three years with the disciples in training them for their work.

Fourth, our cause is the most important in the world. We are charged with the responsibility to preach the gospel to every creature in the world (cf. Mark 16:16; Matthew 28:18-20). This must not be left to chance. We are also commanded to edify those who have obeyed the gospel (cf. Ephesians 4:11-19). Leadership is responsible for leading us to victory in this work.

Fifth, every successful organization recognizes the importance of leadership training. They spend thousands of hours and dollars to insure that their key people will be properly trained. They are not content with last year's training, they must be prepared for the new challenges of today. This is the attitude we need in the church.

Sixth, because of past failures. The history of the church is full of failures because of wrong leadership, or no biblical leadership. We must insure that when they write our history it will not be documented by failure. Leadership must see to it that this doesn't happen.

Seventh, future leaders depend upon today's training. A congregation must not be content because it has a great leadership today. How about tomorrow? Who is being prepared to take these men's place?

Eighth, because tragedy occurs when the "blind leads the blind." This means that we must insure that unprepared leaders won't lead us down the wrong path. A person can't teach what he doesn't know, or lead where he doesn't go; neither can he lead if he isn't prepared.

Ninth, people must be shown as well as told. Leaders must serve as models for followers. This demands preparation as well as demonstration.

Tenth, because behind every plan, goal, or desired work is leadership. A congregation can't work a plan if it doesn't have one; you can't do what you aren't prepared to do.

Eleventh, because an organization is no stronger than its leadership base. If a congregation wishes to serve more people, it must expand its base of organization and ministry. This requires more prepared leaders. The broader the base, the more people you will have involved.

Twelfth, good leadership training closes the gap between the pulpit and pew. As more and more people become involved it will become easier for the pulpit to encourage involvement. Success occurs where everyone knows what you are talking about.

Thirteenth, someone will "take" the lead. It may be good leadership or it may be poor leadership, but it will occur on some level. What we want to do is remove this kind of leadership by replacing it with trained leadership.

Fourteenth, positive and well-prepared leadership develops a positive congregation. Congregations have a tendency to become mirrors of their leaders.

Fifteenth, good leadership glorifies God and exalts Christ. It is living proof that we care enough to train ourselves to be the best we can be for God's work. His work is worthy of every effort we can put forth to become better prepared.

Sixteenth, there has been a lack of leadership training. When was the last time you were in a leadership training class? When was the last time your congregation conducted one? When do you plan to start your next class?

Seventeenth, a lot of leadership methods being used in the church are not the best or fully in harmony with the Bible. Two examples are the board of directors and dictator approach to leadership. Good biblical training will help overcome these problems.

Eighteenth, through leadership training you discover and develop abilities. Many men are preaching today because they discovered their abilities in a leadership training class. Many song leaders and Bible class teachers are active today because of a leadership class they had in the past.

Nineteenth, it provides hope and inspiration for others. One brother stated it like this: "I know our congregation has a great future because we are always training leaders." This attitude should exist in every congregation.

Twentieth, sound doctrine depends upon sound biblical leadership. Through advanced Bible classes, which is a must for leaders, the foundation is laid for supporting the teaching of God's word. A leadership that knows the Bible will not be swept away by every new doctrine that blows through.

Twenty-first, changing times demand creative leadership. Methods that worked 10 or 15 years ago may not be adequate today. It is said that every 10 years now is equal to 100 years of knowledge in the past. This means that if we haven't grown and made changes in our thinking in the past 10 years, we are already 100 years behind. Jimmy Carter, in his inaug-

65

ural, said, "We must adjust to changing times and still hold to unchanging principles." This is a must attitude for the church!

Twenty-second, the success of the followers is the success of the leaders. This gives exciting challenges to leadership. The fruits of one's labor is very rewarding. Proper training increases our "crop." As leadership goes, so goes followship.

Twenty-third, it will make leadership easier and more enjoyable. When you are prepared for a task, you can do it with greater confidence and ease. Nothing is more frustrating than not being prepared for an assignment. Good leadership training insures proper preparation for the job assigned.

Twenty-fourth, it may help some men realize that they are not ready to assume a leadership role. This is just as important as getting men into leadership positions. Many men have never gotten over the shock of being prematurely placed in a leadership role.

Twenty-fifth, it helps us obey Paul's charge. "And the things which thou hast heard from me among many witnesses, the same commit thou to faithful men, who shall be able to teach others also" (2 Timothy 2:2).

The importance of leadership training cannot be overstressed. It is vital to the future of the Lord's church. I hope you will carefully study the 25 reasons and apply them to your life, as well as to your congregation. Why not make plans today for a leadership class or workshop--future generations will be glad you did.

Chapter 2

LEADERS AND PERSONALITY

"I'm not a Mr. Nice Guy, I let the chips fall where they will. If the brethren don't like it, that's just too bad."

It is hard to believe that these remarks were made by a man who was serving as a leader for a congregation. Sadly, they were.

Brother ...... is a great teacher and leader but out of the classroom he can't get along with people on a personal level. His personality is terrible; he is always getting into trouble with people."

These remarks were expressed by a church leader who was discussing another leader who worked with him and why they were going to have to ask him to resign.

I wonder how many leaders have lost jobs because of poor personalities. I venture to say that scores have lost their jobs because of some personality quirk that they weren't willing to correct.

The importance of personality must not be overlooked when discussing the leader. The attitude which expresses that all the leader needs in order to lead is Bible knowledge, is wrong. On this point Henry Greber said, "Our possibilities of success are much more limited by our personality traits than by our intellect." If knowledge insured success, we would expect to see every knowledgeable person, in any field, successful. But this is NOT the case, as you well know.

If you hope to make it as a leader you must work on developing your personality. Concerning the importance of personality, someone has rightly said, "The greatest and most vital power in influencing life is personality. It is greater than law, instruction or example."

No one wants to be like the person of whom it was said, "His personality is like a bent safety pin: It doesn't fit anywhere and is always sticking people in the wrong place."

What is personality? Webster says that personality is the "distinctive individual qualities of a person, collectively. The sum of such qualities as impressing others." Personality is the attitude of a person displayed in actions. The wise man said, "As a man thinketh in his heart, so is he" (Proverbs 23:7). Personality attracts people by producing a pleasing effect. Personality is the display in everyday life of positive qualities and habits. Personality will make or break you. Personality will help you make it as a leader.

One of the most frequently heard phrases used to describe the importance of the leader's personality is, "What you are speaks so loudly, I can't hear what you are saying." Like it or not--admit it or not--personality is powerful.

Check businesses or any other field where people must deal with people, and you will discover that two-thirds of all success depends upon development of a specific group of personality traits, which are positive in nature. The work of the leader is certainly not exempt from this vital truth. The leader is seeking to have a Christ-like personality. This is implied by the word Christian.

When asked what a preacher needs besides his Bible knowledge in order to do an effective work, a veteran preacher replied, "The ability to get along with people in the church, and a positive, friendly, Christ-like personality in all situations."

How does a person get his personality? I don't believe, as some do, that a person is born with his personality. I believe each person develops his/her personality. This is why most persons are lacking in this area: their personality

68

qualities are basically not developed. If a person who has a rotten personality was born that way, and nothing can be done about it, then the Bible is wrong when it talks about the need for CONVERSION. If a person can't change his personality or lifestyle, then conversion is an impossibility. This is false thinking. As someone has aptly put it, "If Christianity has done nothing for your temper, it hasn't done anything for you." And we may add, if it hasn't done anything for your poor attitude or personality, it hasn't done much for you.

I have heard persons rebel against any discussion of improving one's attitude. Some of these were leaders: One brother said, "Personality development is for the birds. I just preach the word and God gives the increase."

PERSONALITY AND THE BIBLE

The Bible is the world's best self-improvement. Therefore, it has a lot to say about the personality of man. There is an interesting example of the power of a pleasing personality in the Old Testament.

The case involves the young man Daniel and his being selected above the "presidents and princes" (cf. Daniel 6:2). Why would a young man, some think no older than 18 or 19, be chosen instead of these older and supposedly wiser men? The answer is in these words, "... Daniel was preferred above the presidents and princes, because an EXCELLENT SPIRIT was in him..." (Daniel 6:3). Thus, one reason Daniel was chosen above the others was because of his pleasing personality. Men are still being chosen for the same reason in our day. If you want to be chosen, develop your personality.

Jesus must have had a pleasing personality. In Luke's gospel we read, "And Jesus increased in wisdom and stature, and in favour with God and man" (Luke 2:52). It is interesting to note

69

that of all the charges brought against Jesus, which of course were unfounded, none were charges that He was rude, crude, antagonistic, belligerent, vehement, etc. In every situation, even when He had to teach and say things that weren't popular, He conducted himself properly. That is why we must follow His example in attitude and action. Christ is the PERFECT personality example.

When the apostle Paul told Timothy to "be thou an example of the believers, in word, in conversation, in charity, in spirit, in faith, in purity," (1 Timothy 4:12), he was encouraging him in areas of personality and relationships to others.

The biblical emphasis upon personality is not based upon looks, a diploma from a charm school, wit, winning a popularity contest, fashions, or some other rare quality. The Bible emphasizes godliness and Christ-likeness as the basis of one's personality. These are qualities that come from within the heart of man. Commitment to these qualities produce such conduct traits as: (1) love (John 13:34); (2) forbearing (Ephesians 4:2); (3) kindness (Ephesians 4:32); (4) consideration of others (Hebrews 10:24); (5) meekness (Matthew 5:1-12); (6) forgiveness (Luke 17:1-5); (7) patience (James 1:1-7); and a host of other qualities which we will be studying later in this work.

ATTITUDE DETERMINES PERSONALITY

Our attitudes are usually expressed in actions. Actions compose a person's personality. Actions are the fruits by which we are known and judged (cf. Matthew 7:16). This is why you must give diligence in developing a positive spiritual attitude. This means that you must study and apply positive qualities to your life, while at the same time removing the negative, destructive qualities from it.

To assist you in developing these qualities, the following attributes are listed for you to study. The positive is stated in the left column and the negative qualities are stated in the right column. Remember the words of the psychologist who said: "Every idea which enters the mind immediately tends to express itself in action."

POSITIVE ATTRIBUTES	NEGATIVE ATTRIBUTES
Love (1 Cor. 13)	Hate
Smile (Prov. 15:13)	Frown
Courage (2 Tim 1:7)	Fear
Gracefulness (Col. 4:6)	Awkwardness
Hard work (Col. 1:10)	Laziness & Indolence
Ambition (2 Tim. 4:7)	No Ambition
Loyalty (Phil. 4:9; Rev. 2:10)	Disloyalty
Optimism (Eph. 3:20)	Pessimism
Tact (1 Pet. 3:15)	Indiscretion
Courtesy (2 Tim. 2:23-26)	Discourtesy
Agreeableness (Matt. 5:25)	Disagreeableness
Kindness (Eph. 4:32)	Harshness
Enthusiasm (Eccl. 9:10)	Indifference
Sincerity (Eph. 6:24; Tit. 2:7)	Insincerity
Wisdom (Jas. 3:17, 18)	Foolishness
Orderly (Tit. 1:5)	Carelessness
Purpose (Phil. 3:12-14)	Irresolution
Decision (Lk. 9:62)	Indecision
Joyful (Phil. 4:4)	Sorrowful
Trust (1 Thess. 2:4)	Suspicion
Cheerfulness (Prov. 17:22)	Gloominess
Open-mindedness (Prov. 18:15,23)	Egotism
Listens (James 1:19)	Interrupts
Calmness (Phil. 4:6)	Anxiousness
Encourager (Prov. 12:25)	Discourages
Self-Control (2 Pet. 1:5-7)	Intemperance

71

Faith (Heb. 11:6)	Doubt
Sympathy (Rom. 12:15)	Severity
Hope (Rom. 8:24)	Despair
Thrift (Lk. 12:16-21).	Waste
Perseverance (Heb. 12:1)	Quitter

The results of the above qualities are far-reaching. Like putting a drop of red dye in a barrel of water, thoughts that are translated into positive qualities of life will have far-reaching affects on the personality. A pleasing personality will have a transforming effect upon your life and work as a leader. A positive personality will "rub off" on the congregation.

How can a person develop these positive qualities in his life? First, he must believe that, with God's help, he can do it. This is positive thinking. From positive thinking comes positive actions: from positive actions comes positive habits. Positive habits produce a positive personality.

A second thing that a person must do is PRACTICE each quality until it becomes an automatic part of daily living. We are told by psychologists that it takes practicing a thing from 17 to 21 times to make it a habit. Once the action becomes habitual, it thereafter comes automatically. It is easy for a smiling man to be friendly. It is easy for a kind person to show kindness. It is easy for a hard worker to keep on working. It is easy for an optimist to see the brighter side of things. It is easy for a gentle person to show gentleness.

Habits, especially new ones, don't come easy. But with resolved determination that leads to practice, habits can be formed. Once habits have been formed, it is easy to keep them. This is true of bad habits as well. This is why we must always be on guard. We are forming and practicing habits almost daily. The challenge is to eliminate the negative and develop the positive. The choice is yours. The day to begin is NOW!

Another thing that will help to develop and keep positive habits is prayer. Daily asking God to help you make the difference. Say, "Father, please help me to be kind today as I come in contact with ....." God has promised to give you wisdom if you will ask for it (cf. James 1:5). "Ask and you shall receive," is what Jesus promised.

As you are working on developing a positive personality remember this truth. Every negative personality can be replaced by a positive one. Go over the list previously given in this lesson and you will see that this is true. Therefore, list the negative qualities that you want to get rid of, and then list the positive qualities that will replace them.

This approach will work if you will put it into practice. Begin today by writing a positive plan of action for developing and improving your personality. You will be glad you did, and others will also be glad.

Remember that 70 to 80 per cent of ALL FAILURES are due to attitude and personality problems.

NICE GUYS FINISH FIRST!

Chapter 3

LEADERS MUST PAY THE PRICE

Recently I was discussing leadership with a brother who trains management personnel for one of the nation's largest companies. During the course of our sharing, he made this statement: "A man must pay the price to reach the top in management or leadership. This price is high. But once he reaches the sought position the price to stay is even higher. Most, however, aren't aware of this truth. They think it will now be easy. Not so. They must work harder, study more, improve their skills and keep on improving to stay on top."

Pay to stay! This is a much needed truth for church leadership too. A man will spend years preparing himself to be a leader (e.g., elder, deacon, preacher, teacher, etc.), and in many cases once he attains it, he tries to coast from that time forward. The needs of the times, as well as the changing times, pass them by. They put the church on hold at status quo. It hasn't entered their minds that the price for getting there isn't the same as the one to stay and function effectively.

As we look around us the evidence is clear that most successful people continue to pay the price. For example, a physician will spend eight to ten years of his life just to get ready to practice. Once his practice has begun, he continues to pay the price through long hours of work, refresher courses, seminars, reading, etc. To be the best he must pay the price.

Should leaders in the church pay a less price? I don't think so because of the nature of their work. They are helping people get to heaven. Thus, their work has eternal value and purpose. Compared to the price our Lord paid for our redemption, our continual preparation for leadership is small.

Through the years I have noted how some leaders like their positions and titles, but spend very little time doing justice to them. In fact, some are even bringing reproach upon themselves and the church. No one is following them and they wonder why. I think there are several reasons why some leaders don't pay the price to stay.

1. They don't realize a price must be paid. Their knowledge of leadership is limited.

2. They aren't really committed to their roles as a leader. It's just something to do.

3. Many don't like the inconvenience involved in improving their leadership skills.

4. Some take any suggestion for leadership study or improvement as an insult or threat.

5. A few leaders are too proud to admit that they need to pay the price to stay.

6. They are lazy and indifferent toward their leadership assignment.

7. Prejudices and mind sets are additional reasons why some don't work on the price to stay.

8. Some feel like they already know everything there is to know about leadership.

9. They would like help and training but don't know how to go about getting it.

10. They simply don't have the energy, motivation or drive to keep on keeping on.

Now that we have noted 10 reasons why some leaders don't pay the price to stay, let's take a few minutes and examine the price leaders must pay to stay.

1. Leaders must pay the price of long hours and hard work.

2. A leader must pay the price of studying and growing in knowledge (2 Timothy 2:15).

3. A leader must pay the price of continually improving his leadership skills.

75

4. A leader must pay the price of accepting responsibility for his actions (Romans 14:11,12).

5. A leader must pay the price of standing firm in seasons of adversity (1 Corinthians 15:58).

6. A leader must pay the price of properly receiving criticism (Proverbs 15:10).

7. A leader must pay the price of accepting the consequences that go with making decisions (Proverbs 16:7).

8. A leader must pay the price of giving up his liberty for the sake of weaker brethren (Romans 14:1-8).

9. A leader must pay the price of tears for God's people and His work (Acts 20:19, 31).

10. A leader must pay the price of self-denial as he follows in the steps of his Lord (Matthew 16:24).

The price to stay! How do you relate to this lesson? Do you feel very encouraged because something has been written about that which you have known all along? Or, are you challenged to "gird up your loins" and tackle your leadership role with a new zeal? Determine to be the best leader you can be for the Lord's church. If you will do this, the best is yet to be!

Chapter 4

LEADERS AND CONTINUING EDUCATION

If the axiom is true, "Leaders are made, not born," then it must also be true that it takes a lot of preparation to make a good leader. A leader in the church assumes his role with a lot of diversity of preparation in his background. His preparation, however, must not end when he is appointed a leader. He must continue to prepare and improve himself for his service in the local church. A good leader will be a continual student of God's word as well as other fields of knowledge that relate to leadership work. This is why continuing education should be of great interest to him.

Millions of Americans are involved in some form of continuing education on an annual basis. The motivation for involvement in such studies are varied. Some are involved because their profession requires it or needs it to insure proficiency, e.g., school teachers, insurance salesmen, doctors, lawyers, real estate brokers, barbers, etc. Others are involved for self-improvements; personal enjoyment; or job promotions. Continuing education plays a vital role in the economical, social, educational, technological, political, etc., successes of our day-to-day life. Everyone benefits from it.

Continuing education is also a vital force in religion. A few denominational groups have developed excellent programs for the in-service training of their workers, especially their ministers. Many of the programs come from special institutions designed for the specific purpose of continuing educational needs. Most of these groups encourage, highly recommend, or even insist that their leaders participate in continuing educational programs on a regular basis. When we come to continuing education among most churches, however, it is easy to see that in most cases it is non-existent on a planned, professional scale. Where it does exist, participation is usually small. The question is why? The answers are many and vary from situation to situation. I do, however, believe that many leaders neglect to participate in an organized or institutionally directed continuing educational program for some of the following reasons.

First, some are satisfied with training and educational accomplishments of the past. Some seem to think that because they finished college (or a course of training) 5, 10 or 15 years ago that this is sufficient for the rest of their lives. And, yet, these same men will readily admit that they have retained very little of the knowledge gained years ago. Some even admit that a lot of the things they studied back then have been of little benefit in their leadership role. The failure of a person to retain, use or be proficient in areas of previous study is further seen in that most colleges and universities will not accept credits over five years old. The basis of this is that the person has probably forgotten most of what he learned five years ago. A servant of the Lord, therefore, must not be content with what happened in the past.

Second, some are too busy to take on the challenge of a continuing educational program. At least this is what they would lead you to believe. While it is true that most leaders "work 25 hours" per day, it is equally as true that they find time to do the things that are important and of interest to them. If continuing education becomes important, they will find time to do it.

Third, some are, sad to say, too lazy to take on the challenge and discipline required for such programs. They appear to be content to just get by, and produce only what is necessary for survival in their leadership assignment. Basically, they are content to drift from week

78

to WEAK! Needless to say, there is no need to go into what the Bible says about laziness: it is a sin!

Fourth, many leaders shun involvement in continuing educational programs because of pride. They seem to think if they become involved it will admit that they are ignorant. And, yet, by their own admittance and proficiency they declare their ignorance in many areas. Only a foolish person will say he has no need to learn because he knows it all.

Fifth, a few leaders fail to take advantage of continuing educational opportunities because of misunderstanding. They see it as the "other fellow's" need, or as a waste of valuable time. Also, some fail to realize that good leadership requires constant learning.

Sixth, many leaders have no personal goals. They seem to have no desire or incentive to embark upon a course of study to prepare themselves for greater opportunities of service. They do not see themselves doing any better fifteen years from now than they are presently doing.

Seventh, many leaders would like to be involved in continuing education but do not think it is possible in their locale. This points to the need for every congregation to provide some type of training for leaders. If this is not possible then plans should be laid to participate in programs held in other congregations, etc.

Opportunities

The acquisition of knowledge comes via many sources and approaches. A worthwhile continuing education program, in order to be beneficial, should provide the opportunity, challenge, resources, and guidance for the student to undertake the learning task and to evaluate his progress toward his objective.

There are many avenues to knowledge. Note carefully some of the following ways a leader may continue his education. First, reading. A person who will read a book or more per week will acquire a great amount of knowledge. This knowledge will increase in proportion to the notes one takes, the amount of review and self-testing he subjects himself to relative to his reading. A thorough reading list, with a variety of subjects on it, is a must for this approach to continuing education.

Second, enrolling in a college or school of preaching. These schools provide excellent opportunities for a leader to learn in a classroom situation. The exchange between student and teacher, as well as between students, will be valuable as a learning aid.

Third, correspondence courses are also a good channel for continuing educational objectives. Many colleges, schools of preaching, etc., offer a variety of courses through the mail. Some also use video and audio tapes with their courses.

Fourth, lectureships and seminars. This has always been an effective means of continuing education for leaders in the Lord's church. Each year many good programs are presented throughout the brotherhood.

Fifth, sharing sessions. This may involve anything from getting a friend to share details about his profession, interest, skill, etc., to planning a definite program for such sessions.

Sixth, special leadership classes taught in the local congregation. This is an excellent way to insure continuing education for leaders. The challenge is for leaders to attend them.

Seventh, leader study groups. This approach consists of a number of leaders in an area getting together on a regular basis to study various subjects. These are very rewarding experiences.

Incentives

From our discussion so far it should be obvious that a number of incentives must be present before a person will become involved in a continuing education program. Some of these incentives are: (1) the need for knowledge in a field or on a subject; (2) personal satisfaction; (3) attaining a goal you started working toward years ago; (4) development of the mental processes; (5) to be a better and more proficient leader; (6) the problems and needs of our changing times; (7) new opportunities will come; (8) it is a good example for others; (9) it is a good habit; and (10) it demonstrates concern and wisdom. Therefore, we must never forget this adage: "It's what you learn after you know it all that counts."

The church leader must be a continual leader, both in the Bible and other vital areas. It is estimated that the average man spends over $200 and 150 hours each year in caring for the outside of his head (e.g., haircuts, shaves, cologne, facials, etc.). Surely we can spend this much on taking care of the inside by filling it with good, usable knowledge. Think about it!

Chapter 5

LEADERS' SELF-RATING SCALE

Someone has rightly said, "There is no greater examination than self-examination." This is true because it helps a person know himself. Through self-examination you come to grips with your weak and strong points. This is essential for great leadership.

Below is a list of statements which relate to leaders and their work. Take a few minutes and answer each one as it relates to you. In the column to the right you will find three possible responses to the statement. Check either YES, NO, or TO SOME EXTENT.

		YES	NO	To Some Extent
1.	I believe leadership training is very important in the church.	___	___	___
2.	I believe each congregation is in its present position because of leadership.	___	___	___
3	I believe the church needs better leaders.	___	___	___
4.	I feel personally needed as a leader.	___	___	___
5.	I believe leaders are born.	___	___	___
6.	I believe leaders come through training.	___	___	___

7. I consider myself a servant leader. ___ ___ ___

8. I believe others consider me a good leader. ___ ___ ___

9. I am aware of the dangers of secular leadership principles being used in the church. ___ ___ ___

10. I am being guided by the Bible in my leadership style. ___ ___ ___

11. I am qualified for my leadership position. ___ ___ ___

12. People find it easy to approach me. ___ ___ ___

13. The church must plan before progress occurs. ___ ___ ___

14. Great leadership demands continual training. ___ ___ ___

15. My weak points won't hinder me from doing a good job. ___ ___ ___

16. I manage my time well. ___ ___ ___

17. I study available material on leadership. ___ ___ ___

18. I daily ask God for help. ___ ___ ___

19. I am willing to deny myself in order to be a ser-

vant leader. ___ ___ ___

20. I understand the nature of total church growth. ___ ___ ___

21. I understand the qualifications of an elder. ___ ___ ___

22. I plan to be the best spiritual leader my talents permit me to be. ___ ___ ___

23. I am for a continual leadership training program. ___ ___ ___

24. I understand and use effective communication tools. ___ ___ ___

25. I find it hard to make decisions. ___ ___ ___

26. I worry about what other people think. ___ ___ ___

27. I don't like to upset people because of my decisions. ___ ___ ___

28. I enjoy team leadership. ___ ___ ___

29. I spend some time each day in Bible study. ___ ___ ___

30. I am a self-starter. ___ ___ ___

31. I understand the biblical mission of the church. ___ ___ ___

32. I know how to delegate. ___ ___ ___

33. I am always working on unity. ___ ___ ___

34. I have an accurate job description of my church assignment. ___ ___ ___

35. I am willing to give up my opinions if they are hindering peace and progress. ___ ___ ___

36. I am willing to abandon faulty leadership principles in favor of better ones. ___ ___ ___

37. I am aware of the dangers of traditions. ___ ___ ___

38. I accept change with ease. ___ ___ ___

39. I understand God's organizational plan for the church. ___ ___ ___

40. I understand that leaders will receive criticism. ___ ___ ___

41. I don't want to be thought of as a dictator. ___ ___ ___

42. I love people and demonstrate it in my actions. ___ ___ ___

43. I am motivated by God's promises. ___ ___ ___

44. I am involved in helping the church grow. ___ ___ ___

45. I believe I must teach the lost. ___ ___ ___

46. I try to be Christ-like in every situation. ___ ___ ___

47. I understand that leadership involves hard work and sacrifice. ___ ___ ___

48. I believe we must prepare leaders for tomorrow. ___ ___ ___

49. I am a leader of deep faith. ___ ___ ___

50. I don't always ask, "How much will it cost" when a work is proposed. ___ ___ ___

51. I am trying to be a good example. ___ ___ ___

52. I believe kindness is an essential leadership quality. ___ ___ ___

53. I put others before myself. ___ ___ ___

54. I am an open leader. ___ ___ ___

55. I am willing to pay the price to be a better leader. ___ ___ ___

56. I would like for our church to try some new methods and programs. ___ ___ ___

57. I am considered by others to be a positive person. ___ ___ ___

58. I have a tendency to follow my emotions. ___ ___ ___

59. I have a biblical concept of leadership. ___ ___ ___

60. I am trying to follow Christ in my every action and decision. ___ ___ ___

61. I am presently involved in a personal program of leadership improvement. ___ ___ ___

62. I daily think of my leadership role and desire for improvement. ___ ___ ___

63. I have a list of personal goals I am working on. ___ ___ ___

64. I believe people find me easy to approach. ___ ___ ___

65. I make friends easily. ___ ___ ___

66. I am not presently upset at anyone in the church. ___ ___ ___

67. I easily admit my mistakes. ___ ___ ___

68. I want to lead the church into the future. ___ ___ ___

69. I will use this self-rating test as a personal growth and motivational tool. ___ ___ ___

70. I pledge myself to be a
better leader.   ___ ___ ___

    To rate yourself, count the number of times you checked YES. This is your positive score. The number of times you checked NO is your negative score. Your doubtful score is revealed by the number of times you checked TO SOME EXTENT. Study your scores very carefully. Determine why you are strong in some areas and weak in others. Do you know why you are doubtful? What do you plan to do as a follow-up to this self-examination?

    Another way to use this rating scale is to have a person who knows you well rate you. How does his rating compare to yours? Also, you may use it to rate someone else. How do you compare to this person? You may also use this scale to rate your church leadership as a whole. In all usage be sure to be Christ-like.

Chapter 6

LEADERS ARE READERS

Through the years in studying and researching leadership, I have been impressed with the fact that, almost without exception, all successful leaders have been readers. I was recently impressed with this fact again as I was reading Richard M. Nixon's book **Leaders.**

Napoleon said: "Show me a family of readers, and I will show you the people who move the world." An unknown person has said: "The man who does not read good books has no advantage over the man who can't read."

I personally believe that a large percentage of leaders in the church don't read as they should. This observation is based upon my experience as an editor, publisher and author. The editor of a popular brotherhood magazine once told me: "...Our people don't read." Why? I am not sure in every case. But I know some don't read because of the following reasons:

Why Leaders Don't Read

1. They never enjoyed reading as they were growing up. One leader confessed to me that he never read a book through during his high school years.

2. Some are very poor readers and shun the frustration involved in trying.

3. Then there are those who feel like they already know enough to stay on top of things.

4. Many leaders must read as a requirement of their jobs; thus, they don't want to spend any of their personal time reading. They are tired of reading.

5. Some say they are too busy to read.

6. A few are lazy and won't put forth the effort to read good books or materials.

7. They don't realize how important it is for them to read and expand their awareness and knowledge.

8. Some are discouraged by others. When they bring up something they have read, they are put down.

9. Many leaders aren't aware of the good material available today. We live in the day of information.

10. Every now and then you come across a leader who thinks it is wrong to read anything but the Bible.

While the leader should read his Bible daily, he must not, however, neglect the reading of other worthwhile books--especially religious and leadership books. Not long ago I was talking with a book dealer and he asked me this question: "Why is it that Christians don't buy books?" As we continued our conversation, I could not help but remember the many times I have asked myself the same question. And even if they buy them, they usually don't read them. Could it be that nonreading leaders are responsible for nonreading followers?

Daniel Webster made a classic statement relative to the importance of religious books. Mr. Webster said, "If religious books are not widely circulated among the masses in this country, and the people do not become religious, I do not know what is to become of us as a nation...If truth is not diffused error will be." To Mr. Webster's statement, I would add that I don't know what will happen to our homes and churches if good literature is not circulated and read. Reading is very important for growth and improvement within the home and church.

Every leader needs a basic library of good books. By reading, studying and sharing the ideas from good religious books, the leader will grow spiritually. This library doesn't have to be very large for it to be helpful. Seneca made a statement worth remembering. "A large library is apt to distract rather than instruct the learner; it is much better to be confined to a few authors than to wander at random over many." This is why we must be very selective in our choosing of religious books. "Choose an author as you choose a friend," is good advice.

H. Mann adequately stressed the importance of books when he said, "A house without books is like a room without windows. No man has a right to bring up children without surrounding them with books, if he has the means to buy them. It is a wrong to his family. The love of knowledge, in a young mind, is almost a warrant against the inferior excitement of passions and vices."

How To Improve Your Reading

There are several basic guidelines that can help a person become a better reader.

1. Develop a deep desire for reading. This will come from a realization of the need and importance of reading.

2. Come to grips with why you don't read any more than you do. Take time to analyze your reading habits.

3. Read some books on how to improve your reading. There are also some good courses available to help persons improve their reading skills.

4. Develop a personal reading plan. Select subjects that relate to your present leadership roles. Set aside some specific time for reading each day.

5. Jot down a few notes as you read. Underline key words or phrases. This will cement your learning of certain key facts, etc.

6. Realize there is a difference in reading for pleasure and studying a text.

7. Form a reading group. This may be composed of leaders or others who enjoy reading.

Meet monthly, or weekly, and share reports on favorite books.

8. Stay abreast of what is available. Secure several bookstore catalogs, and get on a discount bookhouse mailing list.

9. Think about what you read. Imagine various ways a truth may be used in your life or ministry.

10. Practice self-discipline. Reading, if you don't have the habit, will be a challenge.

11. Subscribe to several brotherhood papers. **Christian Bible Teacher** always has a wealth of information for leaders (P. O. Box 1060, Abilene, Texas 79604).

12. Stay balanced. Don't become a book-oholic. Don't spend too much time with your nose stuck in a book.

Chapter 7

LEADERSHIP INTEGRITY AND CREDIBILITY

When a leader loses his credibility he has lost one of his most essential assets. Our nation is just now recovering from the government credibility-gap that was created by Watergate. Trust once lost is hard to regain.

Through his **integrity** a leader establishes his credibility. Webster defines **integrity** as: "a being complete; unimpaired; soundness; uprightness, honesty, and sincerity." Credibility relates to the believableness and reliableness of a person. When the followers no longer believe in a leader, or know they can't rely on him, a crisis is in the making.

How Credibility is Lost

Assuming that a leader once had credibility, and now no longer has it, what may account for this loss? I think there are a number of actions that bring about this loss. Some of the more obvious ones are as follows:

First, credibility is lost through lies. Some leaders, sad to say, have used lies in their dealings with God's people. Even after they have been found out, they continue to hold on to their leadership role; in some cases even without repentance. Actions as well as words are used in lying to God's people. One brother, in frustration, recently said this about a leader: "He rarely tells the truth. He'll lie if it serves his purpose." Liars are promised a severe fate by God (Revelation 21:8).

Secondly, credibility is lost through broken promises. I don't mean a failure to keep a promise because of valid reasons. In such cases the followers usually understand. I am talking about the perpetual practice, like some parents do with children, of making promises with no intention of keeping them. One leader arrogantly said, "promises are to be broken...they'll get over it..."

Third, credibility is lost by failing to follow the Bible. People who love the church know very quickly when they are led in a nonbiblical way. I know a leadership that lost most of their followers because they wouldn't purge sin from the camp as the Bible teaches.

Fourth, credibility is lost by saying one thing and doing another. Consistency is a must for strong leadership. One of the problems with the Pharisees was their saying and not doing (cf. Matthew 23:3). Certainly, leaders make mistakes, but constantly living an inconsistent life is wrong and influences others.

Fifth, credibility is lost through covering things up. The Bible teaches that certain things must occur between persons before it becomes public (Matthew 18:15-20). But sometimes public things are covered up. The real reasons for actions aren't told, or the facts are distorted. This is why wisdom is essential to good leadership (James 1:5). We must provide things honest before all men.

Sixth, credibility is lost through procrastination. This is a very subtle practice which some leaders have developed into a fine science. They will do it, or recommend it be done, at some later date. **Now** is not the appropriate time, however, to do it!

Seventh, credibility is lost by deciding matters beforehand. This leadership play gives the impression that the people really have a say-so in matters, but in reality, things have been decided beforehand. They merely lead the people in a nonmeaningful exercise of "hope" building. Leaders have a right to make decisions "behind closed doors"; but they don't have the right to fool or trick

God's people through such tactics as I've just described.

Eighth, credibility is lost by failing to demonstrate faith. Every Christian must walk by faith and not by sight. When leaders demonstrate a lack of faith by their plans and actions, the followers get very discouraged. Faith must be larger than our capabilities, or the balance in the check book (Hebrews 11:6).

Ninth, credibility is lost through fear and worry. Most followers have about all of these challenges they can handle. They are looking to leaders for courage and demonstration of a positive lifestyle. A fearful leader can't help people be of good cheer (John 16:33), or win over worry (Matthew 6:25-35).

Tenth, credibility is lost through a lack of love and compassion. You can tell in a few encounters if a person really cares about you. Love is a very observable trait (cf. 1 Cor. 13).

Eleventh, credibility is lost through incompetence. You can only "fake" it so long.

Results of Lost Credibility

The twelve points bring to light a number of consequences for leaders who lose their credibility. Here are some specific results of lost credibility!

1. **Resentment:** People resent being taken advantage of and used as puppets.
2. **Rejection:** Followers will not permit you to lead them once they no longer trust you.
3. **Resistance:** They will respond in a negative way to your leadership.
4. **Rebellion:** This is an ungodly consequence that often occurs when people no longer trust a leader.
5. **Retaliation:** Some followers lead a move-

ment to correct a wrong, or challenge a leader through open retaliation.

6. **Regression**: The weak always suffer when there is a credibility problem in the leadership.

7. **Refraining**: People won't support programs set forth by persons who have question marks hanging over their credibility.

8. **Restlessness**: Followers will always be uneasy when they have a leader who has a credibility problem. They usually seek a change.

9 **Retreat**: Followers will usually withdraw from any activities they are involved in; and seek a safe place from which to watch.

10. **Repulsion**: Many followers will have to struggle with overcoming their dislike for a leader who has lost his credibility.

It is very difficult to regain your credibility once it is lost. The challenge, therefore, is to guard it at all cost. Be very careful to avoid all actions and attitudes that would call your integrity into question. There is **ONE** sure way to maintain your credibility. And that is to, in every situation, have the mind of Christ (cf. Philippians 2:5-8). "Guard your heart, for out of it are the issues of life" (Proverbs 4:23).

Chapter 8

LEADERS AND OPENMINDEDNESS

There is a very humorous story about a ninety-year-old man who was being interviewed by a local newspaper reporter. "You have lived here a long time," the reporter stated. "I am sure you have seen a lot of changes in your day."

"Yes, sir!" the old gentleman replied emphatically, "and I was agin' every one of them."

Resistance to change may well be called "hardening of the attitudes." This is a frequent and costly ailment among men. A good case in point is that of an old preacher who said he was always open to new truths and convictions, but that he would like to see anyone who could change him. Too many Christians are like that. Their minds are made up. Their opinions on every subject and opportunity are made up and it is almost impossible to change them.

The classic Bible account of a person who had hardening of the attitude is the story about Pharaoh. Moses had presented sign after sign in an effort to get Pharaoh to let the people go. These miracles were designed to change his attitude and let God's people go. Pharaoh, however, refused to change his mind. "And he (God, jjt) hardened Pharaoh's heart, that he hearkened not unto them; as the Lord had said" (Exodus 7:13).

Even the home can become the victim of hardening of the attitude. Parents who will not consider new approaches and new solutions to their problems, are headed for even deeper conflicts. "I don't need to attend any meetings on the home," is the way one husband and father stated his objection to an invitation by his wife to attend an upcoming seminar on the family. Such attitudes harm the home.

There is nothing more obnoxious than a person

who has hardened his attitude to the point of seeing only two sides to a question: the one he holds and the wrong one. He is so sure of his viewpoint that he can't see any other. Such thinking produces a nonflexible approach to life. Thus, it becomes very difficult to live with a person, or associate with a person, who has a cement attitude. This is especially true when leaders close their minds.

Usually a person who is rigid in his thinking is considered to be a person with a strong personality. But in reality, it usually is a sign of an inner weakness, or insecurity. Thus, a person who hardens his attitudes dares not look at the other side of an issue or question, etc.

One of my favorite examples of openmindedness is the account of the Bereans, which is recorded in the book of Acts. "These were more noble than those in Thessalonica, in that they received the word with all readiness of mind, and searched the scriptures daily, whether those things were so" (Acts 17:11). These people could have easily said, "Our minds are made up!" They didn't, however, and they are remembered today because of their great, positive attitude toward new thoughts (i.e., truth). This is a good example for leaders.

When Paul spoke to the Jews in the synagogue at Ephesus, he encountered hardening of the attitudes: "But when many were hardened, and believed not, but spake evil of the way before the multitude, he departed from them..." (Acts 19:9). Rejection of God's will is the greatest consequence of closedmindedness. The church can't afford to be led by men who practice it.

The miracles of Christ, which were designed to prove that He was the Son of God, were rejected (John 20:30,31) by the people. "For they considered not the miracle of the loaves: for their heart was hardened" (Mark 6:52). Thus, the proverb writer was right on target when he said,

"...he that hardeneth his heart shall fall into mischief" (Proverbs 28:14). A person always loses when he hardens his attitude toward the truth.

Openmindedness, which is the opposite of hardening of the attitude, is not gullibleness. It is a willingness to consider the other person's point. It is knowing that you are not threatened by the possibility of having to admit that you are wrong, and that there may be another side to the issue or question. It is a simple desire to always give the other person a fair chance to state his case, as well as a burning desire to know the truth (cf. John 8:32). Hardening of the attitude is dangerous, therefore, because it is an enemy of the truth.

There are several cures for hardening of the attitude. The first is a realization that you have the problem. Once you have taken the step of acknowledging the problem, you are ready to do something about it.

Second, remember that hardening of the attitude has resulted from years of training your mind to respond in a negative way. Therefore, it is going to take time to rid yourself of the habit.

Third, you must recognize the impact of the words you use. They serve as warning signals to let you know that an "attack of hardening of the attitude" is about to occur. Some of these words are: impossible, can't, limitation, if only, but, difficult, no, doubt, afraid, etc.

Fourth, every day be thankful for the fact that God gave you a brain to use. It is designed for use.

Fifth, try to determine why some subjects close your mind quicker than others. Do you have unresolved prejudices?

Sixth, when you know that you will be confronted with a situation that could close your mind, pray for wisdom to handle the situation (cf. James 1:3-5).

Seventh, always strive to have a balanced

view of life. This means that we allow others the right to think for themselves.

Eighth, don't make a rule that others must always agree with you. A person who always agrees with you is not good company.

Ninth, Paul gives us a sure cure for hardening of the attitude. He prescribes an attitude exchange. He said, "Have this attitude in you which was in Christ Jesus" (Philippians 2:5).

Tenth, by putting the proper information into the mind you will be able to avoid hardening of the attitude. Paul gives us a list of the things that we should put into our minds in Philippians 4:8.

The mind of man is a wonderful thing. Through it we can be happy or sad. From the mind comes the thoughts that determine who we are and what we will do. Through avoiding hardening of the attitude we can have a peace and joy which doesn't depend upon outward circumstances. Therefore, when we free ourselves from hardening of the attitude, THE BEST IS YET TO BE!

Chapter 9

LEADERS AND CHANGE

In a Russian city park many years ago two well-dressed soldiers came each day and took their guard position by an empty bench. The ritual continued for many, many years. Then one day a bright young lieutenant decided to find out why the guards were being stationed daily by the bench. It was not easy to find the origin of this tradition. Finally an old historian came up with this story.

"During the reign of Peter the Great, some two hundred years ago," he explained, "the bench was freshly painted, and the Czar ordered two men in uniform to stand by to prevent men and women from inadvertently sitting on the bench and soiling their clothes. The order has never been rescinded."

If we are not careful in the church, in an age of rapid change, we might find some "empty benches" being needlessly guarded, as we cling to traditions in some congregations. We **must not** be like the fellow who had as his motto, "Come weal or woe, my status is quo."

Before I move deeper into this article let me be quick to point out that the change under discussion has nothing to do with God's word or its faithful application. I am talking about methodologies, programs, traditions, expediencies, etc., which may have worked in times past but may be counterproductive today. There will never be a need to change God's word (2 Peter 1:3; John 12:48). The Bible is our changeless guide in a changing world.

Many leaders find change difficult. Old ways of doing things are comfortable. They are like an old pair of shoes: you hate to give them up. It is not easy to break with traditions and try new programs and methods. Successful leaders are those who have learned to understand and cope with change.

Leaders must keep up with the times. American business spends millions training and retraining people to keep up with the changes that are occurring in our world. Organizations which survive and are growing are those which have learned to cope effectively with the rapid pace of change. This is also true of congregations. Leaders must keep up; if they don't, they will become like old machinery, obsolete. God's message for today's church leader is the same as it was in Moses' day, "Speak to the children of Israel, that they go forward" (Exodus 14:15).

A ninety-year-old man was being questioned by a newspaper reporter. "You have lived here a long time," the reporter observed, "I am sure you have seen many changes through the years." "Yes, sir!" the aged gentleman replied emphatically, "and I was agin' every one of them."

Some church leaders are suffering with a resistance-to-change attitude called, "Hardening of the attitudes." This is a costly ailment and hinders the progress of the local congregation where it is practiced. A few leaders are prone to staying on the same path if they have experienced a few successes in the past. It doesn't matter that the "old approach" is not working today. They don't want to hear any new ideas. When new ideas come up their reaction is "Why?" With the open-minded leader it is "Why not?" Thus, success may become a hazard if it sets our attitudes against consideration of new methods and solutions that threaten to move us from our comfortable pews. Many congregations are "stuckfast" instead of "steadfast" (cf. 1 Corinthians 15:58).

It needs to be pointed out that there are some leaders who are quick to jump on any new method they hear about. They are ready "right now" to get the congregation involved in it. This approach can be dangerous to the stability of the local work. One lady said this about the congregation where she was worshipping, "We never know what to expect from one week to the next. It's like a circus: we're always trying to outdo the last act." All changes should be (1) biblically, (2) prayerfully, and (3) patiently approached. Even then, change will be very difficult for some people. Wise leaders will remember this and pray for wisdom as they lead God's people.

Why Some Find Change Difficult

Planning, organizing, motivating, and leading by church leaders is a continuous process. This process is generated by change and generates change itself. Leadership must plan and organize for change; it must involve the members of the church to enact the change. It is at this point that leaders must be prepared to work with those who will resist change. There is a tendency on the part of many to knowingly or unknowingly resent or resist change. The following list reveals some of the reasons people find change difficult.

1. Where pressure has to be applied to bring about a change there will be resistance.
2. The fear of the unknown is a major reason for resistance.
3. Many resist change because they had a negative experience in the past. They don't want it to happen again. They had rather remain status quo.
4. It is easier to remain status quo. You don't have to do anything.
5. The new might produce failure. They had rather not take a chance on a new approach.
6. They don't understand what the change involves. Where the nature of the change is not clear there will be resistance.
7. It removes an element of security which is contained in the old methods.
8. Many are against change because it is their nature to be negative.
9. Some people practice "reaction" instead

103

of "action." Their emotions override their logical approach to facts.

10. Biblical ignorance. They equate traditions with biblical doctrine.

11. They don't want to deal with the problems and challenges that change brings.

12. It may mean that they have to get involved. They are content with a spectator's approach to Christianity.

13. Some are afraid of what others will think.

14. Where there is a lot of opposition to change most will be affected to resist change.

How to Implement Change

Change, as a general rule, is difficult and even at times a bit traumatic. Leaders must remember that people are shocked by something not expected. Most persons will shy away from any threat to their normal ways of doing things. Even a change in times of worship services can be very difficult for some brethren to accept. When people don't understand an event, program or person, they tend to be resistant to the event or person.

After you have prayerfully prayed about the proposed change, and are sure that it will not violate God's word, you need to use the following keys to implement changes.

First, the major challenge to implementing change is understanding. This is why effective communications are essential. It is only through understanding that people let go of their resistance to change. Research in this area indicates that the greater the understanding of an impending change by those affected, the more readily the change will be accepted. Leaders must work on effective communications with the followers. Do the people fully understand the nature and reason involved in the proposed change?

Second, another key to facilitating change is **involvement.** It is a known fact that people accept change more readily if they were involved in the process of bringing it about. This is why dialogue and interaction among church leaders and members is essential to effective change. Leaders are headed for difficulties if they hand down ideas and projects in an arbitrary manner. Also, don't fall into the trap of asking for participation **after** you have made a decision to change.

When members of the church understand how the proposed change will help them reach the goals set by Christ, they will readily respond to change. This is why leadership must create a positive climate for change. It is not easy, but through work and prayer it is possible.

How do you respond to new ideas?

Chapter 10

LEADERS AND DISAPPOINTMENT

Richard was very excited about being assigned to the congregation's evangelism committee. He spent three months researching a possible mission project for the church. He wrote letters, made phone calls, read literature, attended seminars, and did a lot of other things before he submitted his recommendation. The evening he finally presented his proposal, turned out to be one of the most disappointing experiences in his life. Why? His proposal, after all that work, was rejected by the majority in attendance at the meeting. He was depressed and frustrated for weeks after this incident.

Life is full of disappointments. Shakespeare wrote: "Oft expectation fails, and most oft where most is promised; and oft it hits where hope is coldest, and despair most hits." From those early experiences as children when we didn't get what we expected for Christmas, until today's realization that we have been passed over in the promotion of somebody else, disappointments have always been with us. And yet, for some reason, they are still hard to accept. You would think after all this experience we would now be used to disappointment. However, this is not the case. Each new one that comes our way is a challenge.

Every area of man's life presents him with disappointments. None, however, are more serious and demanding than within the realm of church leadership. By its very nature it contains the elements for possible disappointment. Any time you deal with people and choices you will experience disappointments. This is why good leaders will learn how to properly handle disappointments.

Bible Examples of Disappointment

Webster defines disappoint as: "to fail to

satisfy the hopes or expectations of; leave unsatis-
fied; to undo or frustrate." There are several
Bible examples I believe we are safe in saying
that involve disappointment.

**First, I believe God was disappointed at His
creation.** "And it repented Jehovah that he had
made man on the earth, and it grieved him at his
heart" (Genesis 6:6). How sad! Man who was
created in the image of God was in rebellion.
What a disappointment.

**Second, Moses was disappointed at the nation
of Israel.** Can you imagine how he must have felt
when he came down from Mt. Sinai and saw Israel
worshipping the golden calf? This may well have
been one of the most disappointing days of his
life.

**Third, Jesus must have experienced disap-
pointment.** For example "He came unto his own,
and his own received him not" (John 1:11). The
very people (Jews) who should have known Him
because of their supposed knowledge of the Old
Testament Scriptures, are the very ones who rejected Him. What a disappointment this must have
been. I am sure you can think of many other
occasions where Jesus was faced with disappointment.

**Fourth, the apostle Paul experienced disap-
pointing situations and people.** It must have been
heartbreaking for him to have to say, "Demas has
forsaken me."

**Fifth, the apostle John must have experienced
disappointment.** Tears must have been in his eyes
as he wrote to the church at Ephesus these
words, "...thou didst leave thy first love"
(Revelation 2:4).

If God, Jesus Christ, and other great leaders
in the Bible, were confronted with situations that
caused disappointment, let us not think that we
will be exempt.

Why Some Are Disappointed

The reasons for disappointment are as varied and many as the persons and situations involved in a given situation. What may disappoint one person, may not affect another person. It depends upon a person's attitude and background. Brown wisely wrote: "No man, with a man's heart in him, gets far on his way without some bitter, soul-searching disappointment. Happy he who is brave enough to push on another stage of the journey, and rest where there are "living springs of water, and three-score and ten palms."

Let's take a few minutes and look at some of the major reasons why we become disappointed.

First, some leaders become disappointed because they become too personally involved. A rejection of their proposal is a rejection of them as a person. They can't seem to separate the two.

Second, leaders become disappointed because they place too much emphasis upon a certain program or project. They fail to remember that the sum is larger than the part.

Third, disappointment comes when you care. This is good. Pity the leader who never cares about the Lord's work. L. E. Landon wrote, "How disappointment tracks the steps of hope."

Fourth, if a leader isn't careful he will let pride produce disappointment. Sometimes a leader will stick his neck out on a certain matter he feels sure will become a reality, only to have it fail. We must be careful about the motives behind our wants (cf. Obad. 3).

Fifth, some experience disappointment because they can't stand to lose. Every effort on their part is a personal battle. They want their way no matter what. Obviously, this kind of spirit is wrong.

Sixth, there is always the possibility that you may be wrong. It's okay to be disappointed when this happens. The challenge is to rise above it.

Seventh, because he expects much. "He who

expects much will often be disappointed; yet disappointment seldoms cures us of expectation, or has any other effect than that of producing a moral sentence of peevish exclamation" (Johnson). **Eighth, some are disappointed because followers or other leaders won't go by the Bible.** This is certainly a valid reason for being disappointed. We must always expect what God expects.

How To Handle Disappointment

It takes a big man--a real Christian--to handle disappointment in the spirit of Christ. For a man to experience the hurt that comes from disappointment, and keep it inside, is only possible through the "mind of Christ" (Philippians 2:5-8).

Prayer is another power for handling disappointment. Only God knows what you feel. He is the only one that can provide the comfort you need. He will answer if you will ask (cf. James 1:5-7).

A third key to handling disappointment is the ability to separate rejection of your idea (or project, etc.) from rejection of yourself as a person. It's okay if people disagree with you.

"Man," wrote Bulwer, "must be disappointed with the lesser things of life before he can comprehend the full value of the greater."

Never forget that it may be the case that what we expected and didn't get, may not have been best for us or the church.

When disappointments come, and they will, always be Christ-like!

Chapter 11

LEADERS AND VOLUNTEERS

One of the constant challenges before church leaders is the enlisting and training of people for various works in the congregation. Equally as challenging is a system of accountability once a person accepts a job assignment. This is true because the church operates on the volunteer method in selecting workers.

In Christianity no one is drafted or taken against his will. The Lord's army is composed of all volunteers. Our enlistment began when we denied ourselves by putting Christ on in baptism (cf. Matt. 16:24; Gal. 3:27). This is volunteering for salvation.

The phase of volunteering I am talking about is service (or working) of the Christian after conversion. We usually refer to this as involvement. Webster defines volunteer as, "one who offers to enter into any service of his own free will." I am also using volunteer in contrast to the salaried member on a church staff.

The scenario may run like this. There is a certain work that needs to be done in the congregation. After the need is made known in a meeting or assembly, the question is asked, "Who will volunteer...?" Sometimes there are volunteers; sometimes there are no volunteers.

Biblical Observations

The Bible clearly sets forth the fact that certain works in the church must be done by qualified and appointed men. Elders and Deacons is a case in point (cf. 1 Timothy 3). Even from among these ranks there are occasions of volunteering.

In selecting volunteers it must be remembered that the members of the body (i.e., church) have differing abilities (cf. 1 Corinthians 12:12-27). This means, therefore, that not everyone can do the same thing.

The Bible teaches that each member of the church is a priest (cf. 1 Pet. 2:4-10). This is a fulfillment of Old Testament prophecy (cf. Isa. 61:6). This means that each Christian has a right to approach God in spiritual sacrifices and service. Likewise, every member of the church is both a clergyman and a layman (cf. 1 Pet. 5:3; 2:9). The Bible sets forth as a principle the handicap a novice has because of immaturity (cf. Eph. 4:11-17; 1 Tim. 3:1-7). Thus, certain volunteers must be noted with special care. This is why James warns about being too quick in assuming the position of teacher (cf. Jas. 3:1,2).

In using volunteers we must be careful to stay within Bible guidelines.

Why People Volunteer

Have you ever wondered why a person volunteers? The psychology of volunteerism is a very interesting study; from it a leader can gain some important insights. David Sills writes: "The role relationship most frequently employed in recruiting is that of friendship: 58 percent of all volunteers who were recruited into the Foundation (March of Dimes) were asked by friends." (Glenco, Ill. Free Press, 1958, pp. 110-111).

Eva Schindler-Rainman and Ronald Lippett, in **The Volunteer Community, Creative Use of Human Resources,** writes: "The recruitment process is actually a linkage-process, linking a person who wants to give of himself with an organization that needs volunteers in order to operate; linking a need for self-actualization with an opportunity for experience; linking a need to learn with opportunities for learning; linking a need to be creative with an opportunity to give the most creative service possible" (NTL Institute for Applied Behavorial Science, 1971, p. 65).

It is not possible in every case to know why a person volunteers for a certain work; neither is it essential in some cases. It is good, however, for a leader to have some basic knowledge of why members of the church volunteer. I have documented 15 reasons why Christians volunteer. A person may be motivated by one or more of the following reasons.

1. A sense of duty or guilt. This may be self-imposed or externally imposed.

2. Encouragement by someone else; sometimes in the form of pressure.

3. An emergency need has arisen. The need is NOW.

4. There is a basic desire to serve others, as well as God.

5. Frustrated by way things are being done. Think they can do better.

6. A feeling of confidence in a certain area, or around a specific task.

7. No one else will volunteer. They "have to" or it won't get done.

8. Feeling it is God's will for their life.

9. A belief that they should help or do their part.

10. Some just want to stay busy; they are bored.

11. Some volunteer because they are seeking solutions to their own problems.

12. Volunteers sometimes want to be part of a group. Fellowship is a strong incentive.

13. Some have ulterior motives. They may want to further their political, financial, or social position.

14. Persons volunteer to obtain recognition and status.

15. They must use their abilities.

Guidelines for Selecting Volunteers

These 15 reasons should give the leader some good insights to use as he works with people. In addition to these, there are several considerations that should be given in developing guidelines for

volunteers.
1. Be sure to clearly communicate the nature of the task you are asking to be performed.
2. Try to get the **right** person for the job.
3. Be sure to take into consideration the work and needs of the church.
4. The present priorities must be considered.
5. Ask: What qualities should a person have to do this job?
6. Check the talent and interest profile of each member.
7. Conduct personal interviews with potential volunteers.
8. Have a job description prepared with responsibilities clearly defined.
9. Have a starting and terminating date.
10. Provide proper training if needed.
11. Don't be afraid to say no if a person is not right for the job.
12. Encourage volunteers.

The Lord's church has accomplished great things through the efforts of dedicated people. Volunteers have kept the wheels of progress in motion. Leadership in every generation must do its part in properly handling this great source of power.

Chapter 12

HOW TO FOLLOW THE LEADER

Nothing is more essential to leadership than followers. Obviously, a leader can't lead without followers. From years of study and observation I have concluded that one of the qualities needed to make a great leader is the ability to follow. Some, however, try to ignore this quality in their quest to move ahead in the service of leadership. Even the General didn't begin with a star on his shoulder. Most great leaders were once followers.

The paradox of Christian leadership is that we are both followers and leaders. We follow Christ as well as those who imitate Him; and we lead according to our abilities, position and appointment in the church. We lead by what we **SAY** and **DO**.

Since leaders in the church come from within the membership, learning to follow is a must in preparation for leading. To my knowledge, however, very little is taught about the mechanics of followship. This takes work and a unique attitude, as well as training.

I believe the following tips will help all of us in following leaders, as well as being leaders.

25 Tips On Following

1. Realize the leader is a fellow-member of the Body of Christ. He is your brother and we are servants one of another.
2. Allow him to function in a manner that permits him to do his job. Don't hold him back.
3. Be understanding. Sometimes he has the loneliest or most difficult job in the church. A little understanding is a great source of encouragement.
4. Be open to his approach. This doesn't mean that you have to say YES to every request. Be a good listener.
5. If you have a problem with him, no matter

how great or small, go to him (cf. Matthew 18:15-20).

6. Remember your leaders in prayer. They need them in order to do an effective job.

7. Be patient with them. Not everyone moves at the same pace, or does things like you would do them.

8. Encourage them when you have the opportunity (Hebrews 3:13).

9. Love and appreciate them for their works' sake.

10. Cooperate with them. This is usually the biggest problem between leaders and followers.

11. Be free from jealousy, resentment and envy. Rejoice when a leader accomplishes something for God.

12. Be available. Try to make time to get involved in a task they need you to participate in.

13. Never be against a good work if it is biblical. If you are, you are fighting against God!

14. Be an optimistic supporter of all faith projects (Hebrews 11:6).

15. Remember it is one thing to disagree, and another thing to be a disagreeable person in lifestyle.

16. Study your Bible so that you will know God's will for the church. This helps you recognize "blind leaders."

17. Be supportive of his efforts to lead the church.

18. Always practice the Golden Rule. How would you want your followers to treat you?

19. Don't be surprised if a leader makes a mistake. It happens to the best of men. Doers always run the risk of making a mistake.

20. Do your best to accomplish the job you have been assigned. This makes the leader's job easier.

21. Don't try to "use" a leader because you

are close friends. Respect his authority and decisions.

22. Don't pit one leader against another. Manipulation is not a virtue of Christ-likeness (cf. Philippians 2:5-8).

23. Never forget this rule of life: "You always reap what you sow" (Galatians 5:6-8). Sow positive seeds in your work of following (and leading). The fruit will be enjoyable.

24. Realize that, as a follower, you are part of a team effort. Your contribution is essential to the success of any program of work you are engaged in.

25. Pray for wisdom to be the best follower God would have you be (James 1:5).

God's work is the most important under heaven. It requires leadership skills and followship skills. As these two work together, the church brings glory and honor to God.

Chapter 13

LEADERS MUST EVALUATE

According to an old saying, if you don't know where you are going, any road will do. Likewise, if you don't know how well you are doing, how will you know when you have done the job? This is why evaluation is an important function of leadership. Followers need to know how well they are doing as they work toward congregational goals.

As a rule, leaders do a good job in establishing goals and work plans for congregations. Unfortunately, leaders many times never give any feedback until the end of the year (or program). And in some cases it is only to report the "bad news" relative to failure.

Planning and goals provide the structure and direction for various activities within the local congregation. Plans and goals, however, are not complete if they do not contain steps for evaluating progress. Responsibilities and procedures must be built into the plans. This is a major reason why meetings are held: to evaluate progress. If leaders fail to evaluate, they will not get maximum results from their plans, or be able to make proper changes along the way to insure results.

Plans state what we are going to do. Evaluation tells us how well we are doing in meeting the objectives of the plans. As we evaluate it may be necessary to make some changes in the original plan, or develop a means of removing some obstacles. Every leader must be concerned with "How-are-we-doing?"

I would like to suggest the following guidelines for developing and conducting an evaluation.

1. Be sure to establish dates and guidelines for evaluation in your master plans.
2. The times of the evaluation meetings should be established. As a basic rule, a quarterly evaluation is essential. The nature of the goal

117

will determine the best times.

3. Establish, as much as possible, work-related criteria in the evaluation process. Some appraisals are tied to goal achievement. For example, goal A may be 25 percent achieved at the first quarterly evaluation.

4. Determine who will be responsible for conducting the various phases of the evaluation.

5. Remember that no matter how great a set of plans may appear when they are first established, during evaluation time they may show their weaknesses. Therefore, don't be afraid to scrap them and come up with an alternate plan.

6. Be sure that the evaluation procedure meets the objectives designed for it when it was developed.

7. Be careful about making informal evaluations. A clear set of written guidelines prevents this mistake. Also, be sure that the system is not too complex or it will defeat its purpose.

8. Be sure to have the appropriate facts and figures for documentation during the evaluation. An evaluation is not a guessing session.

9. Be sure that everyone understands the results of the evaluation. Good communication is essential to this end.

10. Each person involved in the evaluation should try to free himself of any bias he may have. The goal is to be as objective as possible.

Your task as a leader will be easier when you include evaluations in your planning. A structured evaluation will insure success in your efforts. Regularly you need to take time to do a complete evaluation of your program your congregation is involved in. It is difficult to examine ourselves, but it is imperative to growth in the Lord's work. When is your next evaluation meeting scheduled?

Chapter 14

CHURCH GROWTH LEADERS

Not long ago I watched with sympathy and a bit of frustration as a community football coach, who was a volunteer, tried to teach a group of boys the fundamentals of the game. It was obvious that he didn't know very much about coaching and football basics. In fact, he later admitted that he was not qualified, but took the job because no one else wanted it.

There are a lot of leaders in the church like this football coach. They have accepted a responsibility but don't know how to accomplish it. This is especially true in the realm of church growth. One leader recently said: "I am on the church growth committee, but for the life of me, I don't know where to begin or what to do." I am sure many men share in this brother's frustration.

Not all leaders are able to lead the church forward in the major areas God desires growth in (i.e., numerical, spiritual, and all others). In some congregations there isn't a leader who has any expertise in the church growth field. In a few congregations there may be one or two who are constantly discouraged because others don't seem to be interested in the subject of church growth.

A leadership team without a leader versed in the fundamentals of church growth is not going to reach its potential for the Lord. A study of church growth reveals a number of qualities in the leadership style of men who help churches grow. These are exemplified through some of the following traits.

1. Church growth leaders seem to have an "obsession" with church growth. They "eat, sleep, talk, and dream" church growth. It is the topic of most of their conversations. You

know when they are around.

2. A church growth leader is a growing person. He is constantly feeding on the Word of God (2 Peter 2:1,2); it keeps his evangelism fires aglow (cf. Jeremiah 20:9).

3. The church growth leader is a knowledgeable person relative to the fundamentals of church growth. He reads and attends seminars to expand his horizons. He knows you can't do something you don't know how to do.

4. Church growth leaders have positive attitudes which are exemplified in their lifestyle. They have removed all negatives relative to the Great Commission from their vocabulary.

5. A dynamic church growth leader is familiar with church history and knows where we are today. He measures every trend in light of the Scriptures.

6. The church growth leader is not afraid to try. He won't let the possibility of failure stop him or the Lord's work (2 Timothy 1:7).

7. Faith is another evident quality in the lives of church growth leaders. They know what it means to walk by faith and not by sight. They trust God's power for victory in every effort to reach the lost.

8. Positive church growth leaders have a world vision. They are able to see beyond the bounds of their church buildings (Mark 16:15,16).

9. Church growth leaders have goals and plans for their lives as well as for the church. They are constantly trying to help the local church set and reach growth goals.

10. A church growth leader constantly prays for the evangelization of the world. This is the burden of his heart which he shares with his heavenly Father.

11. A church growth leader teaches the lost in his world as he has opportunity. He is a soul-winner! He practices what he teaches others to do.

12. Church growth leaders aren't afraid to make decisions to grow. They know there will be resistance, but they decide to move ahead as God has commanded.

13. Church growth leaders understand the mission of the church. They are not sidetracked with the minor or supportive works of the church. Souls are first! Every program is measured with this question: How can this help us reach the lost?

14. Church growth leaders are servants. They resist the "executive" approach to God's work. They don't desire to function as "order givers" or "work supervisors." They follow Christ and want others to do likewise.

15. Church growth leaders are loving, patient, understanding and kind. They know people don't change overnight or easily.

16. A church growth leader never stands in the way of God's work. He will never "vote no" for church growth programs that are biblically based, even though he may not be qualified to participate.

17. Church growth leaders study and analyze their situation. They know that no other congregation has the same mixes as their congregation. What works in one church may not work in another church.

18. Church growth leaders believe the world is lost without Jesus Christ, and that the gospel is the ONLY power unto salvation (cf. Romans 1:14-16). It is the DUTY of the church to evangelize the lost!

19. Church growth leaders know that people grow churches. Programs are merely aids to an end and must not become the ends within themselves. People are more important that programs.

20. Church growth leaders realize the dangers of materialism. They are deeply aware of the Laodicean lethargy that may hinder or kill church growth.

21. Church growth leaders look for ways a thing can be done; not for reasons why it CANNOT be done.

22. Church growth leaders don't close their minds or eyes to new ideas. They are open to new possibilities for church growth. They hear the full story before they make a decision.

23. Church growth leaders are not looking for "success guarantees" before they will begin a program. They realize that faith is the real key to success.

24. Church growth leaders try to enlist others to work with them. They realize that it takes a "functioning body" to get the job of world evangelism done.

25. Church growth leaders are not content with status quo. They know this is the first step toward decline.

How about you? Are you a church growth leader? Is there a church growth leader on your team? How many of the attributes in this lesson describe you? Would you like to be a church growth leader? You can begin today by dedicating yourself to this goal. Take these twenty-five attributes and examine your life and leadership style. Commit yourself to a leadership study program; determine you are going to become an "expert" in what God has set as the priority for the church: GROWTH.

Chapter 15

LEADERS AND PROGRAMS

Do you have any idea how many programs have been inaugurated and later abandoned during the history of the congregation you are presently a member? Programs, like people, come and go; yet, God's desire to make disciples of all nations remains unchanged (cf. Matt. 28:18-20).

Almost without exception, every congregation is in search of good, workable, biblical programs for church growth. Through reading books, attending workshops and seminars, the search goes on. Surely, somewhere the right program exists.

It is generally hoped that the application or adaptation of one of these programs will ensure new interest, growth and forwardness in the local church, as well as in the lives of each member. Thus, program after program is copied, yet the congregation never seems to do very much toward achieving their potential, or reaching the heights of congregation A, from whom it was acquired. Oh, they may experience a little change or growth, but frustration soon sets in; the program is abandoned. On the search goes; somewhere, hopefully, the "perfect" program must exist.

Some leaderships like to change preachers with marked frequency. One leader admitted he liked this approach because with the coming of a new preacher there was also the advent of new ideas for programs. "We've got to keep fresh programs," he replied, when asked why they encouraged such a practice.

During nineteen years of preaching I have seen a lot of programs come and go. I have copied a few, as well as originated a few. Because of my experiences I have developed a list of basic reasons why borrowed programs, that work well in one congregation, may not work well in another congregation.

1. The real philosophy, mechanics and nature of the program may not be completely understood. Some move too quickly in adopting new programs.

2. In some cases the leadership is not prepared to properly handle the program. This is vital in borrowing programs.

3. Members don't fully understand the program or their role in it. Thus, they aren't sold on it. Proper communication must ensure that everyone has been informed.

4. Your context (i.e., socio-economical conditions) may not be the same as the church you are borrowing from. A big city program probably won't work in a rural community(?).

5. The biblical basis for the program may be questionable. Just because someone else is successfully doing it doesn't guarantee it is right.

6. Proper education and preparation has not been completed.

7. The congregation doesn't have the right talent-mix to implement and maintain the program.

8. It may merely be a fad that has died and is being resurrected by an uninformed novice.

9. The program may not be working as well as you think. Zeal and the quest for new programs can blind us to some key factors if we're not careful.

10. The program may serve only to inflate the adaptor's ego, and have no real sustenance for the church's future.

11. Your congregation may not be spiritually, financially, or numerically able to handle the new program.

12. The same degree or amount of **faith** required for the program's success is not available in your congregation.

We've noticed 12 reasons why a borrowed

program may fail in a congregation. However, I think there is a deeper reason why borrowed programs have such a hard time in being adapted. As we search for programs, we are, as a general rule, starting in the wrong place, we are looking without instead of within.

The beginning of church growth is within the heart of each member. This truth is exemplified in the Parable of The Sower in Luke 8. The master church builder said: "But that on good ground are they, which in an honest and good heart, having heard the word, keep it, and bring forth fruit with patience" (v. 15).

Along with this truth goes these words of James: "But be ye doers of the word, and not hearers only, deceiving your own selves" (Jas. 1:22). Before any congregation can grow the members must be motivated from within their hearts to **DO** the Lord's will. This motivation will come from the realization that we are redeemed and have a labor of love to perform. Thus, as Jesus, we must be about our Father's business, seeking to save that which is lost.

Good leaders develop good programs. But they must be careful not to substitute anything for the real drawing power in church growth. What is it? Jesus said, "And I, if I be lifted up from the earth, will draw all men unto myself" (John 12:32). Christ lifted up is the drawing power! Let's keep him "lifted up."

Are you in search of a good program for church growth? Why not go back and restudy the book of Acts. It is the record of how the church in the first century successfully carried out her mission given by Christ (cf. Mark 16:15,16; Col. 1:23). Its principles will work in the twentieth century, too. If we will but "continue steadfast in the apostles doctrine and fellowship, and in breaking of bread, and in prayers" (Acts 2:42), we shall turn the world upside down. Let's copy their program!

Chapter 16

LEADERS AND MEETINGS

"There will be a short business meeting after services are dismissed. All men are asked to please attend. It won't take very long." Have you ever responded to an announcement like this, only to find yourself two hours later still sitting in the "short meeting"? Most of us have been involved in some of these so-called "short meetings" which wasted hours of our valuable time.

Meetings, contrary to the dislike that some people have toward them, are essential to the welfare and progress of the local congregation. Most meetings, however, waste a lot of time because they aren't properly planned and efficiently conducted. Thus, they become real time wasters. Why is this true?

10 Timewasters

There are several major reasons why meetings may waste a lot of valuable time.

1. **Some meetings are called for a vague purpose.** No one seems to know why it was called; in some cases not even the person who is in charge of it. Every meeting needs to have a clearly defined purpose for being called.

2. **Many meetings digress into chit-chat sessions.** Some men don't have any opportunities to express themselves, tell their jokes, or have dialog during the normal routine of their lives. Thus, the business meeting becomes a "town social."

3. **Meetings drag on because of the domino or boxcar principle.** One subject touches another subject which leads to another subject, ad infinitum. In the end you are 180 degrees away from where you started or wanted to go. A good meeting is like a train: it stays on track.

4. **From time to time there are persons in the meeting who don't need to be, or people who should be there are missing.** The **right** people are essential for a productive meeting. Time can be wasted when the person, for example, who has the facts or authority is not present.

5. **A poorly prepared agenda, or no agenda, ensures time will be wasted.** If possible, send a copy of the agenda in advance of the meeting. During the meeting be sure to stick with the program.

6. **The location (i.e., place and space) may cause a lot of inconvenience, distraction and waste of time.** This plays a vital role in the success or failure of a meeting.

7. **Most meetings aren't started on time and never end on time.** It is not right to delay a meeting because some have chosen to arrive late. Some think there is a special virtue in going on "eternally" with meetings.

8. **The atmosphere of a meeting will determine how productive it will be.** All meetings have a "feeling";, it's obvious as you are in it. It should always be positive for best results. Negative meetings waste a lot of time.

9. **If the leader (e.g., chairman) of the meeting isn't prepared to properly conduct the meeting, trouble and time waste will occur.** These skills must be learned and used for effective meetings. **Robert's Rules of Order** is a must.

10. **Cut-and-dry meetings waste time.** When things have been decided before hand, it is a waste of time to bring people together and play games with them. Such approaches lead to discouragement, frustration, and a desire not to attend any more meetings. Honesty is still the best policy!

What Is a Business Meeting?

In a word, it's an expedient. To this, however, additional remarks need to be added.

It is a prayerful time of considering the many areas of work carried on by the local church. It may be an elders', deacons' preachers', members' or any combination thereof, meeting for a specific purpose.

Things just don't happen. It takes planning, vision, work, discussions, decisions, examination, etc., to move the local church forward for the Lord. A well-organized meeting will help accomplish these objectives.

Reason For Attending

Sure, a lot of business meetings haven't been what they should have been. That doesn't mean, however, that they can't become more productive. Here are six basic reasons for a person to attend a meeting of the church (assuming he should be there).

First, because you are an important member of the church. Paul points this out in 1 Corinthians 12:13-27. The Body, if it is to properly function, must have the strength and activity of EVERY member.

Second, because the business to be discussed is the greatest business in the world--God's business. In the everyday business world, meetings are held by the thousands to discuss the temporal affairs of life. The business of the church is more important than all these combined, because souls are involved.

Third, because you have a chance to be heard. We hear a lot today about what is wrong with the church. Some of those doing the complaining won't lift a finger to do anything about it, or attend meetings so they can speak out and offer suggestions to help the church grow.

Fourth, because it lets the Lord and others know that you care. Like it or not, many brethren view those who do not attend business meetings as unconcerned about the Lord's work. It's difficult to convince someone you care about the church when you don't support its programs, or attend special meetings.

Fifth, because it will encourage others. We all need encouragement. Whether the meeting is called by the men in a congregation without elders, or whether it is called by the elders, it's encouraging when people show up to support the effort.

Dos and Don'ts

1. Do determine if there is an alternative to having a meeting.
2. Do have a specific purpose for the meeting.
3. Do inform the participants well in advance of the date and time.
4. Do send an agenda.
5. Don't invite persons who aren't needed.
6. Do set a time limit on your agenda. Give only so much time to each item. List the amount by each item.
7. Do start on time.
8. Don't get sidetracked.
9. Don't waste time on nonrelated issues.
10. Don't go over the allotted time.
11. Do assign a responsible chairman, as well as a timekeeper.
12. Do keep accurate minutes and make them available as soon as possible to those in attendance.
13. Do follow-up. This involves progress reports, as well as decisions.
14. Don't allow interruptions. Only an extreme emergency.
15. Do be prepared. If you have something to share or a report to make, have it ready; use only the time allotted. If possible have handouts.
16. Don't attend the entire meeting if you aren't needed; leave when your contribution is over.

17. Don't talk just for the sake of it. Have something important to say.

18. Do maintain the "mind of Christ" (Phil. 2:5-8).

19. Do pray for wisdom (James 1:5).

20. Don't waste your time attending irrelevant meetings.

Meetings are a must for a growing church. If planned and properly conducted, great things can come from these efforts. As a leader you should prepare yourself to be a positive contributor in each meeting you attend. The remarks in this lesson are designed to help you in this area. Study them carefully; or better yet, why not study them as a group. In this way everyone will benefit from this material.

Chapter 17

LEADERS MUST REMEMBER NAMES

An effective quality of a good leader is the ability to remember names. For most of us, however, this presents a demanding challenge, because we haven't given much thought to improving in this area.

Have you ever wished for a pill, or something, that you could take that would help improve your memory? If you have, I have some encouraging news for you. The newest report by the psychiatric researchers at the National Institute of Mental Health opens the door to a memory pill that people could take before exams, to recall names and telephone numbers and to better perform skilled tasks. But before you get too excited and rush out to buy some of these pills, Dr. Herbert Weingartner of the NIMH's Laboratory of Psychology and Psychopathology said, "Perhaps in five or ten years we may have a chemical that can improving learning and memory."

This means, therefore, that if I want to improve my memory I am going to have to take another approach. The only one I know anything about involves work. But it's worth it; especially when it involves remembering names and faces.

There are two familiar statements, that if followed, will take you way down the road to success. Here they are:

1. "There is nothing sweeter to a person's ears than the sound of his own name."
2. "Everyone wants to be remembered. One sure way to know that he is, is the assurance that you remember his name."

If you want to be a success, start early learning people's names and call them by their names. It will pay. It is a pleasant reward to see a person's face light up when you call him by name; especially when he doesn't expect it, or thinks you don't remember it. It's like the child in New Haven, who started the Lord's prayer: "Our Father which art in New Haven, how do you know my name?"

In his book, **God's Psychiatry**, Charles Allen states the feelings of many when he describes a teacher who did not take the time to learn his name. "I had a professor in college one year who never did learn my name. Somehow I never liked him very much."

Of Jesus, our perfect example, it is said, "He calleth his own by name" (John 10:3). If you're like me, you like this statement. I am not lost in a crowd; or just another face among many. My Lord knows my name! I can never know everyone like the Master did (or does), but I can do my best to remember people and their names. This will help me become a better leader.

I would like to share a few basic principles that have helped me to remember names. I do not profess to be an "expert," because I fail from time to time in this important area of public relations. The following suggestions are worth reading and trying if you are interested in remembering names.

Things To Avoid

Before I present the positive principles for remembering names, I want to call to your attention a few things you should avoid while trying to develop your ability to remember names.

First, rid yourself of the "I just can't remember names" attitude. As long as you feed your mind with this kind of self-talk you won't be able to remember names. Tell yourself over and over these words: "With my desire and God's help, I WILL remember people's names."

Second, remember there is not a magic formula that can guarantee that you will remember the names of every person you meet today. I recently witnessed a "memory expert" fail to remember several names in his routine at a motivational seminar. It happens to the best of us.

Third, avoid complex memory systems. In a number of memory training books the authors recommend conjuring up ridiculous mental pictures involving objects (or names) to be remembered. Sometimes this approach backfires. A good example is the man who tried to remember Mr. Rose's name by picturing him a large, rose nose. The next time he met Mr. Rose, he confidently said, "How are you, Mr. Nose?"

Fourth, don't try to remember too many names at once. Concentrate on a few at a time. Usually the "sideshow" approach to remembering names lasts for a few minutes. The challenge is to really remember names tomorrow or next week.

Fifth, don't become discouraged. Remembering names is work. However, it is worth the time and effort, because it lets people know you are really interested in them.

Sixth, don't fall into the trap of approaching remembering names as a game. The word will get out, and your effectiveness will suffer, as well as your integrity. No one wants to be the object of someone's ego trip.

Seventh, don't procrastinate. If you want to remember names, today is the time to begin. You can do it. The key is don't wait for a better time. It will not come.

Some Keys to Remembering Names

There are scores of suggestions in print on how to remember. I believe the following will zero in on the basics that are essential for remembering names.

First, determine that you really want to remember names. This is half the battle. Once this decision has been made, the rest will come easy.

Second, be sure that you have heard the name clearly. A good way to do this is by using it three times: (1) when you meet the person, (2) during a conversation, and (3) when you say goodbye. Repetition is the key to all memory work.

Third, associate the face with the name. Review the association through review. A good help is writing the name down. This will implant the name deeper in your memory.

Fourth, if the name is unusual ask the person how to spell it, or pronounce it. He will appreciate your interest in his name.

Fifth, try to associate the name with a context. Where does the person work? Where did you meet? Who are his friends? Where does he live? What are his hobbies?, etc.

Sixth, don't try too hard to recall a name. Psychologists tell us we store 10,000 bits of information in our brain every second. Take your time. The name will come if you have really taken the steps to remember it.

Seventh, be name-conscious. Always think names and how important it is to remember them.

Eighth, concentrate on remembering names. It is a discipline which requires work. Stop, look and listen with all your concentrated effort.

Ninth, look the person in the eyes (or face). Focus your attention on facial features that will help you recognize the person later.

Tenth, remember this truth: The more you work on remembering names, the easier it will become. Don't quit!

Eleventh, when it's hopeless, don't bluff. Be honest and admit that you don't remember the name. Ask for it again. This shows that you are trying.

Good luck as you apply these suggestions for remembering names. THE BEST IS YET TO BE!

Chapter 18

LEADERS MUST RECOGNIZE DIFFERENT GROWTH RATES

One of the most inspiring accounts of conversion in the New Testament is the teaching and baptizing of the Ethiopian Eunuch by Philip. The book of Acts reveals that after his baptism "he went on his way rejoicing" (8:39). Why all this rejoicing? His sins were forgiven and he was now a free man in Christ! He was on his way back home with the Good News of Christ.

I have often wondered what it must have been like when the Eunuch reached his homeland and began to share the news of his conversion. How was he able to make it as a one-of-a-kind person in a "hostile" environment? How was he able to grow without a spiritual straightjacket being placed upon him by the brethren to keep him on the "straight and narrow"? How could he have succeeded without proper regimentation of his daily life and the practice of a checklist religion?

Becoming a Christian means that a new relationship has been established between God and man. The child of God has become a new creature in Christ (2 Corinthians 5:17); he is a disciple (learner) who is in the process of developing his **unique** abilities in Christ (cf. 1 Corinthians 12:13-27). This, according to the Hebrew writer, takes time (Heb. 5:12-14). New Christians, according to Peter, are "babes in Christ" (1 Peter 2:1,2), and need a special diet and care from the mature members of the Body (cf. Ephesians 4:11-16).

Just as in physical growth, there are no shortcuts to spiritual maturity, as some of our brethren are trying to bring about in some congregations. In fact, to hear some talk, and read their writings, you are led to believe that

135

producing mature Christians is possible through an assembly line approach in discipling: i.e., put every new Christian through the same program, demanding identical activities from each one, etc., and you have a sure method for the new convert to grow by.

Leadership is responsible for recognizing, and acting accordingly, that each Christian grows at his own pace. You cannot force everyone to grow at the same rate.

I believe the assembly line approach to making disciples is contrary to the tenor of the New Testament's teaching on Christian growth. Such an approach sets up unnecessary hurdles for the new Christian to "jump." In some cases it is no more than just another form of legalism, which can squeeze the very joy and individuality out of the Christian life. Any system that produces one standard model of "good, orthodox, properly behaving, do the same thing, only way to please God" approach to Christian growth, is not a position that is in harmony with the New Testament Epistles. Didn't Jesus teach that a man is ONLY responsible for using what he has? (cf. Matt. 25:14-30).

The straightjacket approach to Christian living is not biblical. Definite boundaries are placed on one's life by the Scriptures, but, within the limits, the Christian has the latitude to grow and develop his own uniqueness. No one has a right to bind upon God's servants any other approach to living (cf. Romans 14:10-14).

The assembly line approach to Christian growth denies the possibilities Jesus spoke about, when He said: "I have many things to say unto you, but you cannot bear them now" (John 16:12). Some brethren teach today that a new convert must be ready to do everything they are told to do; there is no room for growth or better understanding. If you are converted, you must do it now.

136

The assembly line approach to growth makes a **workaholic** out of the child of God who is dead to the law by the Body of Christ (cf. Romans 7:1-7). He is placed into a system which demands that he do a "101" things in order to prove his faithfulness to the Lord. If he ever finds himself with any free time on his hands, he feels guilty. He must always be moving and doing. He dare not try to follow the example of Jesus and the disciples in Mark 6:31, where Jesus said, "...come away yourselves...and rest a while." A workaholic is in bondage. He works out of duty instead of joy and love. He always wonders if he is doing enough to maintain God's favor.

Another problem I see with the assembly line method of so-called spiritual growth, is the **overemphasis** it places on intellectualism. It leaves the impression that the one who knows the most is the most spiritual. This is the same problem the Gnostics had, as they sought to encourage others on to a "higher knowledge" which would bring salvation. Bible doctrine is essential for growth, but its meaning becomes real in the life of a Christian as he "studies to show himself approved unto God" (2 Timothy 2:15), and prayerfully applies it to his life as a "doer of the word" (James 1:21-23). Growth in knowledge does not signify maturity in and of itself; maturity comes when your faith is tested and you pass the test through the power gained from God's word (cf. James 1:2-7; Ephesians 6:17). As a doer of the word I have as much right to determine how I will use it in my life as anyone else. And who is to say that my application, to my unique situation, isn't the right one?

Any approach to Bible study, and application of the truths gained, that uses it as a sledge hammer to beat others into conformity is wrong. A good example of this is how some use Romans

14:21: "It is good neither to eat flesh, nor to drink wine, nor any thing whereby thy brother stumbleth, or is offended, or is made weak." This verse is used to goad new Christians into conformity. They are told that they must attend...; or not do this; be sure to take time for this; don't wear this, etc., because if they fail it may offend a weaker brother. When you take time to check on who is really offended, it is not the weaker brother but the **stronger** brother who is offended and raises objections. And on it goes!

James reminds us of the wrong of trying to judge and censor one another in the church. "There is one lawgiver, who is able to save and destroy: who art thou that judgest another?" (James 4:12). When a brother seeks to impose a list of "thou shalts" and "thou shalt nots" upon another, that are not contained in the biblical text, he is in serious trouble with God. It is wrong to reject the commandments of God in order to keep your own traditions (cf. Mark 7:9). The Lord has not called us to produce spiritual job descriptions for one another so that we will be able to know when to pray, study, visit, etc. All of these things are good and will probably be present in one form or another in every Christian's life as he grows in Christ; they emerge slowly through maturity and should not be imposed artificially.

The answer to the assembly line approach to discipleship is elders and evangelists doing the work assigned to them by God (cf. Ephesians 4:11-16). As these men follow the Bible, as well as show by their lifestyle, new Christians will be led into the "fulness of Christ." There are no shortcuts. It takes time! If you doubt this statement, take your Bible and read the accounts of how long and hard it was for men like Peter to mature in Christ. Let's be patient with God's children!

I know of a case where twins, growing up in the same home, eating the same food, etc., are different in weight, height and looks. This also happens in the spiritual family. This is why leadership must constantly work on developing growth programs that fit the needs of the members. One program won't fit every need; one time frame won't be long enough for everyone. Therefore, respect and relate to differences (cf. 1 Corinthians 12:14-27).

Chapter 19

PERSONAL EVALUATION
FOR LEADERS WHO TEACH

Of all the tools or opportunities the leader has at his disposal, none is more powerful than teaching. In one way or another, all the great leaders in the church have been teachers. The Master of course was the perfect teacher. He taught as one with authority and not as the scribes or pharisees. Our goal should be to imitate our Lord, by being the very best teacher we can be.

Teaching is one of the most rewarding and responsible positions in the church (cf. Ephesians 4:11-16). Through teaching, the teacher seeks to influence persons for time and eternity. This is why a person dare not take the job of teaching lightly. James wrote, "Be not many of you teachers, my brethren, knowing that we shall receive heavier judgment" (James 3:1). These words should cause every teacher to stop from time to time and reflect upon his life and teaching. Personal evaluation is a must for the teacher of God's word.

There are many ways for a teacher to examine himself/herself. To assist you in a quick self-evaluation, I have prepared the following inventory for your usage. It will help you zero in on your performance as a teacher. It also contains an incentive factor; you are asked to set a goal in each area for the next two months. In the slot you are asked to place an "N" (Now) to confirm your present position and an "F" (Future) to establish the position you wish to be in after two months.

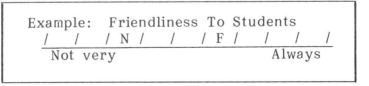

1. I fully understand my responsibilities as a teacher.

   / / / / / / / / / /
   No   Totally

2. I understand my task is to help mature my students in the Lord.

   / / / / / / / / / /
   Not at all   Fully

3. I have a good understanding of my students' needs and wants.

   / / / / / / / / / /
   Very little   Complete

4. I use the best teaching methods to reach my class members.

   / / / / / / / / / /
   Never   Always

5. I am always fully prepared for my classes.

   / / / / / / / / / /
   Never   Always

6. My lesson objectives are always clear and written down.

   / / / / / / / / / /
   Never   Always

7. I set a good example for my students in and out of class.

   / / / / / / / / / /
   Never   Always

8. I attend all worship services of the congregation.

   / / / / / / / / / /
   Never   Always

9. I constantly try to improve my teaching skills.

/ / / / / / / / / /

Never   Always

10. I always arrive early for my classes.

/ / / / / / / / / /

Rarely   Always

11. I pray daily for my class members.

/ / / / / / / / / /

Rarely   Always

12. I make home visits to every member of my class.

/ / / / / / / / / /

Rarely   Often

13. I promote and attend class social activities.

/ / / / / / / / / /

No   Frequently

14. I know each member of my class on a personal basis.

/ / / / / / / / / /

None   All

15. I attend workshops and teacher training sessions.

/ / / / / / / / / /

Never   Often

16. I read books, magazines and other materials on teaching.

/ / / / / / / / / /

Never   Regularly

17. I have a regular program for personal spiritual growth.

/ / / / / / / / / /

No   Regular

18. I work on keeping my students interested in the subject I am teaching.

/ / / / / / / / / /
Never   Always

19. I make my students feel comfortable in class.

/ / / / / / / / / /
Never   Always

20. I strive for variety in my teaching methods for a lesson (e.g., lecture, discussion, question-answer, reports, projects, films, charts, etc.).

/ / / / / / / / / /
Never   Always

I hope you have found this evaluation beneficial. For maximum benefits, I suggest that it be used in a teacher meeting where feedback from others can assist you in setting goals for the next two months. You will be a better teacher if you will follow through with a positive plan of action based upon your personal evaluation.

Chapter 20

DON'T SURRENDER YOUR DREAM

"Today we sailed on." This entry is found time after time in Columbus' daily log. It is the key to his discovering the Americas.

America landed a man on the moon because she wouldn't forfeit her goal. Teamwork turned the dream into reality.

Edison, the Wright brothers, Ford, and thousands of others accomplished great things because they wouldn't surrender their dreams.

The dreams, visions, promises and teachings of the Prophets were never surrendered, because God was fulfilling a promise to fallen man (cf. Genesis 3:15; Matthew 1:21; Galatians 4:4).

Christian leaders must not surrender their dreams (1 Corinthians 15:58).

Press On!

Press On! Though mists obscure
The steep and rugged way,
And clouds of doubt beset,
Soon dawns the brighter day.

Keep on! Though hours seem long
And days deep-fraught with woe,
Let patience have her perfect work
And vanquish every foe.

Hope on! Though all is lost
And storms beat high.
Have faith! Be still and know
That God is nigh.

--Unknown

The disciples of the first century were given the mission to "preach the gospel to every creature" (Mark 16:15, 16). They faced every possible form of persecution:

1. Opposition by friends	5.	Rejection
2. Prison	6.	Ridicule
3. Poverty	7.	Hatred
4. Banishment	8.	Death

Did they surrender their mission? NO! The gospel was preached to every creature under heaven in their lifetime (cf. Colossians 1:23).

You, as well as every leader in the church, have a dynamic purpose for being alive. You have been given a mission by God. It is 10-fold in nature:

1. To glorify Him (Ephesians 3:21).
2. To bring Him pleasure (Revelation 4:11 kjv).
3. To serve Him (Luke 6:46).
4. To obey Him (Hebrews 5:8,9).
5. To co-work with Him (1 Corinthians 3:9).
6. To do good unto all men (Galatians 6:10)
7. To disciple others (Matthew 28:18-20).
8. To live faithfully and godly (2 Peter 1:3;; Revelation 2:10).
9. To bear fruit (John 15:1-9).
10. To encourage others (Hebrews 10:24).

Your 10-fold mission involves daily commitment and work. It functions when you are about the Father's business, endeavoring to have the mind of Christ (Philippians 2:5-8).

Beware of the F's of Surrender

Satan, the world, and even friends and brethren, don't merely use one or two tactics in trying to get us to surrender our mission, goals and dreams in life. F is for FAILURE, and that's just what Satan, and others, want to see happen in our lives. There are at least twenty-two failure tactics that people use on us, and we use on ourselves, in attempting to get us to surrender our dreams and leadership roles.

Don't ever surrender your dreams or mission

in life! Beware of the following mission aborters.

1. **Don't surrender to force.** People will try to pressure you into quitting. They will laugh at you, threaten to withdraw support, and warn you of terrible things that will happen if you continue. Be like Nehemiah and tell them to "bug off." You're not going to surrender your dream!

2. **Don't surrender to fear.** This one will get you quicker than any other. "What if it won't work?" "Suppose the people say no." Fear is a sin and is a major enemy of faith. God hasn't given us a spirit of fear (2 Timothy 1:7).

3. **Don't surrender to facades.** These are fake, imaginary obstacles that sidetrack us, and may eventually lead to surrender. Don't let phony things sell you on giving up your goal. It's always too soon to quit!

4. **Don't surrender to foes.** The leader of all foes, is the king of foes, Satan. "Be sober, be vigilant; because your adversary the devil, as a roaring lion, walketh about, seeking whom he may devour" (1 Peter 5:8). He tried to stop Jesus (Matthew 4:1-6); he will try to stop you too. He works through people.

5. **Don't surrender to freeze.** Don't get in the middle of your mission, having discovered some great challenge, and then get cold feet and quit. "Whatsoever thy hands find to do, do it with all thy might."

6. **Don't surrender to fantasies.** Some people live in an unrealistic dream world. Their goals and aspirations are unreasonable and out of touch with reality. A person with an 80 IQ will never be a brain surgeon. You can't do anything you want to do, or be anything you want to be. That's reality!

7. **Don't surrender to frolic.** Fun, play and games keep some people from ever reaching their goals. A balanced life is vital to accomplishing your goal, but given to a pursuit of fun leads to failure. Work is the royal road to success.

146

8. **Don't surrender to factions.** Sometimes small groups, or several persons, will try to divert you from your goal (1 Corinthians 1:10). Don't give in to a special interest faction (Ephesians 4:1-7). You and God constitute the majority.

9. **Don't surrender to fickleness.** Don't change your goals every time the weather changes. Know what you want, and what God wants you to do, and then move ahead. "Whatsoever thy hands find to do, do it with all thine might.

10. **Don't surrender to the Future.** The, "Oh, I'll wait until tomorrow and then I'll get started," attitude is a loser's way of procrastination. "Say not that there are yet four months, and then cometh harvest? behold, I say unto you, Lift up your eyes, and look on the fields; for they are white already to harvest" (John 4:35).

11. **Don't surrender to fate.** This trusting luck or a nebulous thing called fatalism. What God has commissioned us to do is possible. Your destiny is not controlled by the stars or horoscope.

12. **Don't surrender to fever.** At the least rejection or setback, some people get "boiling mad" and give up their mission. Anger is a positive emotion that must be controlled. Paul wrote, "Be ye angry and sin not."

13. **Don't surrender to fences.** We all live within fences we have built within our minds. These are self-imposed boundaries: e.g., "It's not time yet"; "I don't know enough"; "I don't have the assurance I need," etc.

14. **Don't surrender to faces.** When you share your dream with another person, he frowns, laughs, or makes fun of you. Don't let facial expressions stop you. Don't wait for approval before you begin. When the world boo's you, bounce back.

15. **Don't surrender to finances.** "I don't have the money"; "It costs too much"; "What if we can't pay for it?"; and "Where will we get the money?" The other side of the coin is when people quit for more money.

16. Don't surrender to feelings. This is where negative emotions take over and cause us to relinquish our dreams. Discouragement, depression, worry, fear and many other feelings move us into the inactive zone. Don't give in to your feelings. Go by the facts!

17. Don't surrender to a farce. This is a lie that you let influence you. Satan says we can't do it. God says we can. "Ye shall know the truth and the truth shall make you free" (John 8:32).

18. Don't surrender to frustrations. Success is never easy. Anything worthwhile will have challenges and setbacks. Wait until the frustration passes before you decide to quit.

19. Don't surrender to fables. These are the traditions that say such things as, "You can't teach an old dog new tricks," or "Opportunity only knocks once."

20. Don't surrender to failure. Most people have failed more times than they have succeeded. Almost everything was failed when it was first tried. Don't let guilt or worry about past failures stop you. Learn from your past mistakes and move ahead.

21. Don't surrender to fog. Fog is a dense hindrance to vision and progress. You can't see far. This is where the walk of faith takes over: "We walk by faith and not by sight."

22. Don't surrender to forts. Fences keep you in, and forts keep you out. Some people see every door with a "Keep Out" sign on it; they believe there is not a way to get in and enjoy the "goodies" of life. If you have faith as large as a grain of mustard seed, you can move mountains. Charge the fort!

Don't surrender your:

1. mission
2. dream
3. goal
4. leadership

5. purpose
6. hopes
7. possibilities
8. faith

to these twenty-two enemies of positive leadership.
Dare to dream. Dare to act upon your dream,
and whatever you do, don't surrender your dreams.
This is the sure way to failure. God's leaders
don't give up! Through team efforts dreams are
kept alive and accomplished.

Chapter 21

BOLDNESS: A MUST FOR LEADERS

Hiding behind closed doors! That's the last place you would expect to find a group of men who had been selected to change the world. But that's where we find the disciples of Christ after His crucifixion. "...when the doors were shut where the disciples were assembled for fear of the Jews" (John 20:19a). This fear, however, subsided because Jesus came and stood in their midst "and saith unto them, peace be unto you" (John 20:19b).

What a difference Jesus makes when He comes into a situation. Things change. Negatives turn into positives. Cowardice becomes courage. Fear shifts gears and moves forward. Worry turns to winning. People become bold in the face of foes.

Since our plea is restoration of New Testament Christianity, and since our plea is to follow the Bible in all things, then it's imperative for us to restore the spirit of boldness in our evangelism and daily living. A timid, scared spirit won't preach the gospel to every creature. We must be sold on being bold. "For God hath not given us the spirit of fear; but of power, and of love, and of a sound mind" (2 Tim. 1:7).

Webster defines bold as "showing a readiness to take risks or face danger; daring; fearless." The Hebrew word (**batach**) means "to be confident," and the Greek (**tarrheo**) means "to be warm, zealous, daring."

The German playwright and poet, Johann Wolfgang Goethe, wrote:

Are you in earnest? Seize this very minute;
What you can do, or dream you can, begin

it; boldness has genius, power, and magic in it. Begin and then the work will be completed.

Boldness in Acts

"We make way," wrote Bovee, "for the man who boldly pushes past us." A look through the book of Acts reveals the spirit of boldness in the lives of first century Christians:

Now when they saw the boldness of Peter and John, perceived that they were unlearned and ignorant men, they marvelled; and they took knowledge of them, that they had been with Jesus (Acts 4:13).

And now, Lord, behold their threatening and grant unto thy servants that with all boldness they may speak thy word (Acts 4:29).

And when they had prayed, the place was shaken where they were assembled together; and they were all filled with the Holy Spirit, and they spoke the word of God with boldness (Acts 4:31).

And he spoke boldly in the name of the Lord Jesus, and disputed against the Grecians, but they went about to slay him (Acts 9:29).

Then Paul and Barnabas waxed bold, and said, it was necessary that the word of God should first have been spoken to you...(Acts 13:46).

And he began to speak boldly in the synagogue...(Acts 18:26).

And he went into the synagogue, and spoke boldly for the space of three months, disputing and persuading the things concerning the kingdom of God (Acts 19:8).

Wouldn't it be great if the church of today restored the spirit of boldness? The Proverbs writer penned: "The wicked flee when no man pursueth; but the righteous are bold as a lion" (Prov. 28:1). Bold as a lion! Does that characterize your life and ministry?

Why be Bold?

• We must be bold because we have a bold message: "The gospel is God's power unto salvation" (Rom. 1:14-16).

• We must be bold because we have a bold Master: "...and, lo, I am with you always..." (Matt. 28:20).

• We must be bold because the opposite, cowardice, is a sin (Rev. 21:8).

• We must be bold because our enemy, Satan, is bold (1 Peter 5:8).

• We must be bold because it attracts others (Acts 4:12).

The church needs leaders who will lead her boldly into the strongholds of Satan and capture hearts for the Master. Such actions will require bold strokes in methodologies, stewardship, and commitments. Timid, retreating spirits won't win the world for Jesus.

Our people must be trained to live boldly in an ungodly world. The world must be brought UP to our standards instead of us going DOWN to its standards. It takes nerve to live holy and righteously in this world (cf. 1 Peter 1:15,16).

When people laugh, ridicule, threaten, and

try to stop us, we must say with Nehemiah, "...Now therefore, O God, strengthen my hands" (Neh. 6:9).

The keys to boldness are basic:
B - Believe
O - Obedience
L - Love
D - Dedication

We must **believe** in God, His promises and power to see us through every obstacle: "Greater is he that is in you than he that is in the world" (1 John 4:4).

Regardless of the circumstances, we must be **obedient** to the Lord's will: "Though he were a son, yet learned he obedience...he became the author of eternal salvation to all them that obey him" (Heb. 5:8,9; cf. Luke 6:46).

Love is the greatest: "There is no fear in love, but perfect love casteth out fear; because fear hath torment. He that feareth is not made perfect in love" (1 John 4:18). Love makes us bold.

Dedication must be complete. Jesus said, "...if any man will come after me, let him deny himself, and take up his cross, and follow me" (Matth. 16:24).

Restoration is incomplete until we have restored the spirit of **boldness** in the life of every Christian. Once this has happened, they will take note that we, too, have been with Jesus. Let's be sold on being bold.

Boldness

When fear takes over, it
Saps joy from your soul.
It's a negative enemy who
Robs you of your positive goal.

153

There's a solution to winning
Over this negative foe;
Affirm in your heart that
You'll always be bold.

Boldness is ordained within
God's holy writ;
All the great persons
Of faith won through it.

Boldness is a state
Deep within your mind;
It's a positive friend
Who'll always treat you kind.

So when fear comes
And seeks to leave you cold.
Tell it to go because
You're sold on being bold.
                    (J. J. Turner)

The Church, perhaps as never before, needs men of courage. There are no shortcuts to boldness. Boldness is a vital ingredient for building an effective leadership team. All the truths learned from the study of this book require a spirit of boldness for implementing.

The Boldness Pledge

God being my helper, and the Scriptures being my guide, I _____,
                    (Name)
pledge myself to being a bold leader for the cause of Christ.

_____
                    (Signature)

Make No Small Plans

Make no small plans,
They only accomplish small things.

Make no small plans,
They have no power to excite.

Make no small plans,
They don't require our very best.

Make no small plans,
They demonstrate small faith.

Make no small plans,
They only interest small thinkers.

Make no small plans,
They require little creativity.

Make no small plans,
They leave us comfortable and satisfied.

Make no small plans,
They don't attract big dreamers.

Make no small plans,
They require only nominal commitment.

Make no small plans,
They extract very little energy.

Make no small plans,
They don't attract attention.

Make no small plans,
They turn off people who love a challenge.

Make no small plans,
They give a false sense of accomplishment.

Make no small plans,
They aren't in harmony with our mission.

(J.J.Turner)

Other Books
by J.J. Turner

Growth Through Biblical Stewardship
Called To Be Champions
Sermons You Should Preach
Positive Christian Living
God's Way to the Top
Winning Through A Positive Spiritual Attitude
How To Win Over Emotions
The Book of James
How to Turn Your Dreams into Realities